082
O s2s

68619

DATE DUE			

THE STUDENT LIFE

SIR WILLIAM OSLER

THE
STUDENT LIFE

AND OTHER ESSAYS

by

SIR WILLIAM OSLER

With an Introduction

by

H. H. BASHFORD, M.D

Essay Index Reprint Series

BOOKS FOR LIBRARIES PRESS, INC.

FREEPORT, NEW YORK

082
Os 2 s
68619

First published 1931
Reprinted 1967

January, 1970

THE FRONTISPIECE

is reproduced from the portrait painted by John Sargent in 1905 of " The Four Professors," and now in the possession of Johns Hopkins University, Baltimore. The original includes—

W. S. HALSTED, Professor of Surgery,

W. H. WELCH, Professor of Pathology,

W. OSLER, Professor of Medicine,

H. A. KELLY, Professor of Gynæcology,

all of Johns Hopkins University.

"The address entitled *The Student Life* has been reprinted by permission of the Estate of Lady Osler, and with acknowledgment to Messrs. P. Blakiston's Son and Company, from the late Sir William Osler's *Aequanimitas*."

CONTENTS

FOREWORD

IN the year that Queen Victoria came to the throne, there sailed from Falmouth a young married couple. The husband, grey - eyed and sturdily built, was the Reverend Featherstone Osler, the son of a Falmouth merchant and the descendant of a long and respectable line of traders. For some years he had served in the Navy, attaining the rank of sub-lieutenant, but, leaning towards the Church, had exchanged this for Cambridge, whence he had been ordained a few weeks earlier. His wife, who was slender and dark, but physically strong—she was destined to see her hundredth birthday—had been a London girl living for some time with an uncle in Falmouth ; and the two had become engaged about three years before, soon after Featherstone had left the Navy. They had looked forward to a quiet country living, but there had recently been pressed upon them the necessities of Canada,

the almost complete dearth of any organised
spiritual influence in the outlying English
settlements of Ontario and Quebec—not yet
christened as such and still known as Upper
and Lower Canada respectively—and being
both ardent and adventurously inclined had
at once decided to go there.

With all their worldly goods, therefore—
not very much, but including, we are told,·a
tin of a particular local confectionery—they
had embarked ; and seven-and-a-half weeks
later they duly arrived in the St. Lawrence.
In the history of Canada it was an uneasy
period. It was true that the American inva-
sion of seventeen years before had evoked,
for the first time, a spirit of colonial unity.
But local jealousies were strong, and even
bubbling into armed conflict. In Lower
Canada, still predominantly French and
Catholic, the seigneurial system was dying
hard, while its Protestant immigrants looked
askance at the official policy of religious
tolerance. In Upper Canada, which had
largely been populated by loyalists driven
north after the War of Independence, the
newer comers from the English manufac-
turing towns, the crofts and cabins of Scot-

x

land and Ireland, were being looked down upon and occasionally treated as a somewhat inferior kind of interloper. The boundary between Nova Scotia and the American State of Maine was still undelimited and a matter of acute controversy ; and west of the Great Lakes as far as the Pacific, over a continent still regarded as incapable of agriculture, the Hudson's Bay Company, with its scattered traders, was the only representative of civilisation. There were no railways. The cost of sending a letter to England was some three or four shillings ; and although four years earlier the first Canadian-built steamer had crossed the Atlantic, the million and a quarter people who formed the total population—chiefly concentrated, of course, in the eastern provinces—were living more or less precariously upon the land as farmers, lumbermen and trappers.

Such was the Canada in which the Oslers found themselves, landing in the first instance at Quebec, where they were warmly welcomed by Bishop Mountain, the second Protestant Bishop of the diocese. Thence, by way of Kingston, they proceeded to Toronto, and after a two days' journey by road arrived at the little settlement of Bond Head and their firſt Canadian home. This consiſted, they found, of two tiny rooms, a sitting-room and bedroom, with a barn for the luggage, upon what was then the verge of a largely unsettled and primeval foreſt. The neareſt poſt-office was twelve miles away, the neareſt doctor fifteen, the surrounding farms had juſt been hewed, or were ſtill being hewed, out of the timber; there was no church, and it would have been difficult to conceive a greater contraſt between the reality and the setting that they had been picturing for themselves, only a few months before, as the probable scene of their married life.

Besides their own youth, however, and the happy gregariousness that their family was later so abundantly to share, there were other influences to aid them. The neigh-bouring settlers of all denominations seem to have been resolved to give them their chance, and, having summed them up, came to their help in a very practical way. Within a short time a couple of churches had been built, some seven miles apart, and a rather more adequate dwelling provided to serve

xii

as a rectory. For the young minister it was less of a home than an occasional sleeping-place between arduous journeys, but for the settlement as a whole, thanks to his wife, it was soon the centre of a score of activities. In spite of the birth of two healthy babies, she had established classes for the surrounding children. And when, at the end of four years, a temporary breakdown necessitated a holiday for the family in England, there were waiting to welcome them on their return no less than sixty waggon-loads of people, who insisted on accompanying them from the nearest landing-place throughout the twelve miles to the rectory.

It was the sort of tribute that must have been an ample reward for a second farewell to the comforts of England ; and for the next sixteen years they remained at Bond Head, nine children being ultimately born to them. Of these, William was the sixth son ; and by this time—he was born in 1849—Bond Head could boast of a schoolhouse, a doctor, and some two hundred inhabitants. Moreover, there had settled in the neighbourhood two or three more families of gentle birth and education, and the Oslers' rectory with its growing brood of generous, sporting and quick-witted children, had already gathered these into its arms and was busy initiating them into the life of the community. From the material standpoint this was still a struggling one, and the rector's portion of it was no exception, although he had acquired a small farm upon which the elder boys had already begun to work in their spare time. Mrs. Osler's way, too, of disposing of her infants during her busier hours seems to have been a simple one ; and we read of the future Sir William at the end of a tether, sharing a peg with one of the calves.

Financially regarded indeed, as many years afterwards he was to confess to one of his audiences, his particular outlook at this time could scarcely have been called an auspicious one, " born seventh," as he explained, " in a missionary's family, in the backwoods of Ontario, with twins ahead." But then, as he might have added, it was no ordinary family—not in the sense, perhaps, of accumulating wealth, but of being able to prove, given the right spirit, how little this matters to the finest sort of achievement. Thus, of the barelegged boys running about

xiv

the farm, the eldest was to become a Justice
of the Court of Appeal of Ontario ; another
—B.B., as he was affectionately called—the
leading Queen's Counsel in the Dominion ;
a third, Edmund, the President of the Dominion Bank of Canada and a Director of
the Canadian Pacific Railway ; and himself
the Regius Professor of Medicine at Oxford,
and one of the best-known physicians in
the world.

Of Osler's school days it can probably be
said that they were those of the majority of
backwoods youngsters, although a certain
element of mischief, which was never quite
subdued in him, seems to have perturbed
some of his earlier teachers. It at any rate
led to his removal from the school at Dundas,
whither his parents had migrated in 1857,
and it is to be feared that he left his next
school upon the shores of Lake Simcoe not
wholly regretted by those in charge. But
at Trinity College School, Weston, near
Toronto, to which he was sent at the age
of sixteen, he was lucky enough to meet
and be profoundly influenced by a very
remarkable man.

This was Father Johnson, its warden—the

school was an Anglican one moulded on English lines—a devout High Churchman, but also a scientist, and especially a naturalist, of infectious enthusiasm. Here, for the first time, Osler came under the spell of the microscope and, scarcely less formatively, of Sir Thomas Browne, of whose *Religio Medici* he was later to possess a copy of every edition issued up to 1850. Looking back, indeed, it might be said that these were the twin stars of his life, although to his own world, at this time, he was no more than an average schoolboy—not very big, but a good all-round athlete, with lively, rather deep-set, brown eyes, and the curious almost Indian-brown complexion that he had evidently inherited from his mother. Even in his own mind his future was not yet decided, and when, in due course, he proceeded to Trinity College, Toronto, it was with the general intention of studying theology and following in the footsteps of his father.

At Toronto he was to meet, however, the second and even more potent of his life's earlier influences in the shape of Dr. Bovell, the chief organiser of the Toronto Medical School. He had been deeply moved, too,

xvi

by the revolution in thought just initiated by Darwin and Huxley, and by the autumn of 1868, in his twentieth year, he had definitely enrolled himself as a medical student. Afterwards he was to become supreme as a general clinician, teacher and writer. But his initial approach to medicine was naturally determined by his love of microscopy and the study of natural structures ; and he might very easily, in his first years, have drifted into the career of a pure biologist just as a little later he might have become—and probably would have done in a succeeding generation—a whole-time pathologist, devoted to the elucidation of post-mortem and morbid tissues.

Probably, in the end, it was his love of people, and particularly of bedside teaching, that settled matters. But throughout his years of apprenticeship he remained in close touch with Father Johnson, spending many of his holidays collecting and examining and annotating specimens for his former schoolmaster. In 1870 he entered McGill University and obtained his first insight into practical medicine as a clinical student in the wards of Montreal General Hospital. This was then, as he afterwards described it, " an old coccus- and rat-ridden building," in which both surgical and medical cases were haphazardly treated in the same ward. But it was in Montreal that Osler met Dr. R. P. Howard, the third of his youth's great friends and mentors; and having at laſt found his true vocation he put every ounce of himself into his work. In faɕ, " Lazarus was nothing," he once wrote to his siſter, " to what I have been for the laſt three weeks "; and two years later he had taken his M.D. with a special prize for his thesis. This, charaɕteriſtically, had been accompanied by thirty-one microscopic and other preparations, and the whole had been ſtamped, as his examiners agreed, with originality and research.

That was in 1872, and since his qualification had found his purse almoſt empty, the next few months, from the ſtandpoint of his later career, were of a somewhat critical nature. The temptation to earn money, to sacrifice a problematical future for an immediately lucrative present, muſt have been a ſtrong one, although to the end of his life he cared very little for personal wealth. But

xviii

happily his brother Edmund, who had just become engaged and was planning a visit to Scotland to see some of his future relations, conceived the idea of asking William to accompany him, and generously offered to pay his expenses. It was typical of the family. It gave Edmund just the companion that he wanted. And for his younger brother it was to prove the first of a life-long series of similar journeys. For, having enjoyed the hospitality of his brother's hosts and visited Dublin, Edinburgh and Glasgow, he made his way to London, where for the next fifteen months he studied physiology under Burdon Sanderson. He also enlarged his acquaintance with the writings of Coleridge and Lamb ; soaked himself in the art and architecture of England—" though we could put the whole island," he enthusiastically wrote home, " into one of our lakes, yet there is more local interest in one parish than in the whole of our Dominion " ; took his licentiate of the Royal College of Physicians ; spent some months in Vienna and Berlin ; returned to London again and Burdon Sanderson, whom many years later he was to succeed at Oxford ; listened to Canon

Liddon at St. Paul's ; toyed with the idea of entering the Indian Medical Service ; refused a Lectureship in Botany at McGill ; and finally, in 1874, came back home with a whole new world of friends and experiences. Wisely for himself, too, if not for his pocket, he had remained uncommitted to any form of practice ; and it is interesting to note that it was not until his return that he earned his first medical fee—fifty cents for removing a speck of dust from the eye of a patient in Dundas.

He was then apparently assisting a local practitioner. But in July, thanks to his work abroad, he received the offer, which he decided to accept, of a Lectureship in Physiology at McGill University. Monetarily it was a very modest one, and we learn from an early account-book that he hired a room for two pounds a month, spending another eight upon a ton of coal, a desk, chair and bookcase. Of the lectures themselves, however, let a contemporary speak. " They began," he wrote, " with an explanation of the old Edinburgh term Institutes of Medicine. Then, in a bold outline, he sketched inorganic and organic matter, vegetable and organic life, vital force, and closed with a description of cellular life and an outline of future lectures. From that hour physiology was an attractive study and the lectures like unto gods."

That may have been an exaggeration on the part of a student, listening for the first time to a new note not only in Canadian but, as was afterwards to be made manifest, in American university life. But it is no exaggeration to say that they marked the beginning of the renaissance of McGill University. By the end of a year, and at the age of twenty-six, Osler had been raised to the status of a Professor, and temporarily obtained charge, during an epidemic of small-pox, of his first beds in the Montreal General Hospital. He took the disease himself, but only mildly, succeeded in amplifying his income by a hundred pounds, and spent the greater part of it in equipping his physiology class with some fifteen microscopes. Better still, at any rate in his own eyes, he had proved his worth as a clinician, and the following year was made pathologist to the Hospital and given command of the post-mortem room. Here again he introduced new methods, and within twelve months of his appointment had collected notes of a hundred thoroughly systematised examinations. He had also started a medical society amongst the students for the informal discussion of cases, and in the year 1878, although not yet thirty, was made full physician to the Hospital.

This was over the heads of three assistant physicians—an inexcusable promotion, as he afterwards smilingly admitted—but it can be regarded as certain that, if it caused any heartburnings, these were of the briefest duration. Heads may have been shaken, as they undoubtedly were, over some of the young physician's idiosyncrasies—his antipathy to drugs, for example, of which he was congenitally suspicious, and of which, in his own practice, he was remarkably sparing. There were always occasions, too, never quite predictable, when his irrepressible humour would come to the surface either in his own person or the vicarious shape of one Egerton Yorrick Davis. This gentleman, so his creator alleged, was an ex-American Army surgeon, who had sojourned for his sins amongst various remote and unpronounceable Indian tribes. Here he had observed and would sporadically report the most astounding medical cases, one of which actually appeared, to its editor's subsequent confusion, in a responsible technical journal. Oftener he would write, in a not altogether unfamiliar hand, to Osler's friends and acquaintances, and in later years, to the perplexity of journalists, would occasionally represent him in hotel registers.

But neither envy nor malice could live in Osler's presence; and he was soon busy within the hospital bringing about changes comparable with those he had already initiated in the university. " He began," wrote one of his fellows, " by cleaning up his ward completely. All the unnecessary semblances of sickness and treatment were removed; it was turned from a sick-room into a bright, cheerful room of repose. Then he started in with his patients. Very little medicine was given. To the astonishment of everyone, the chronic beds, instead of being emptied by disaster were emptied rapidly through recovery; under his stimulating and encouraging influence the old cases nearly all disappeared; the new cases stayed but a short time."

Prior to this he had made another brief trip to England in order to take his membership of the Royal College of Physicians, and included a visit to Edinburgh, where he made the comment that " Listerism " did not appear to be making much headway. Unlike Lister, indeed, he was curiously slow in recognising the enormous significance of Pasteur's work—probably on account, as his friend and biographer, Professor Harvey Cushing, has suggested, of the hold still exerted upon English medicine by Bastian's theory of " spontaneous generation." Nobody was ever franker, however, in acknowledging his mistakes or readier to explore a new avenue ; and in 1881, when he attended the International Congress of Medicine held in London under the presidency of Sir James Paget, he had the opportunity of hearing Pasteur in person explaining his theories and results. He still remained, perhaps, not wholly convinced. But when in 1882 came the discovery of the bacillus of tuberculosis, he fully realised, with all its implications, the advent into medicine of bacteriology.

Meanwhile he had come to be recognised not only as the most inspiring teacher but

one of the ablest physicians in Montreal, and
in 1883 he received the honour of being made
a Fellow of the Royal College of Physicians.
In the next year he again visited Europe,
meeting in Berlin Koch, the discoverer of
the tubercle bacillus, and while still abroad
he was offered the Chair of Medicine in the
University of Pennsylvania at Philadelphia.
Taken by surprise and devoted to Montreal,
he decided at last that he would toss for it,
and was sufficiently strong-minded, when the
coin indicated Philadelphia, to abide by the
result. Not until he returned, perhaps, was
he fully to realise the depth of feeling that
his decision had caused—a degree of regret,
almost amounting to consternation, amongst
his fellows at McGill University. But the
die had been cast, not wholly by himself, he
would probably have been mystic enough to
believe ; and at the age of thirty-five—he
had been a professor for nine years—he bade
a final farewell to his work in Canada.

So began, in the October of 1884, what
was to be the richest period of his life, the
twenty years that he spent in the United
States, divided between Philadelphia and
Baltimore. By the end of them he had be-

come, though none the less British, the best
beloved doctor in America—a consultant by
whom, if he would only consent to come,
almost any fee could be commanded; who
would travel all day and most of the night,
without any fee at all, to help the obscurest
colleague; whose home was synonymous
with the wisest, gayest and most disarming of
hospitality; and whose text-book had become the portal through which almost every
English-speaking student was entering the
profession of medicine. As at Montreal,
however, so at Philadelphia, there were at first
a few natural criticisms. For one thing, the
young Canadian, with his informal garments
—lectures at Philadelphia had hitherto been
extremely dignified—his easy attitude upon
the platform, lounging against a wall or
sitting upon a table, and his superficially un-
impressive delivery, was entirely contrary to
established precedents. But through the
everyday manner the matter of his teaching
was quickly perceived to be anything but
commonplace, and his methods of individual
bedside instruction were a revelation to his
new students.

Moreover, here as everywhere, his transparent modesty, harnessed though it was to a tremendous driving-force, forbade enmity even from those seniors who had deplored his appointment as a stranger. He was soon, indeed, to make amongst them some of his closest friends, including Weir Mitchell, the famous doctor novelist, and Mr. and Mrs. Gross, the former being the son of America's foremost pre-Listerian surgeon, and the latter the great-granddaughter of the Paul Revere hymned by Longfellow for his midnight ride. His ability had begun to be recognised, too, on the other side of the Atlantic. In the year 1885 he was invited to come to England to deliver the Goulstonian Lectures. And the handling of his subject, Malignant Endocarditis, was such as to reveal him instantly as a teacher of the highest order. It was the first really broad, clear and thoroughly documented account of a not uncommon, but hitherto vaguely recognised, form of cardiac disturbance. It at any rate stamped him upon the English mind, a little contemptuous of Colonial and American medicine, as a man of whom any university in the world might not unreasonably be proud.

For four years Osler remained at Philadelphia, throwing himself as usual into the student life, establishing new laboratories, and beginning to undertake a limited amount of private consulting work. Unlike most of his colleagues, who at that time were also engaged in general practice, he made it a rule, as he had done in Montreal, to be a consultant in the strictest sense—only to see patients, that is to say, who were brought to him, or whom he was invited to visit, by their own doctors. Amongst these latter, as it chanced, was Walt Whitman, in his little two-storey frame house at Camden, the lower part of him buried, as Osler has described it, under a mass of papers, books and manuscripts, and his face "lost in a hirsute canopy" of snow-white hair, beard and moustache. Of *Leaves of Grass*, Osler wrote that "it was not for my pampered palate accustomed to Plato, Shakespeare, Shelley and Keats," and deeply as he came to admire Whitman the man, he never seems to have been attracted by his verse.

But other eyes were upon the Canadian professor and his work at Philadelphia. Thanks to the munificence of a Quaker millionaire, there had come into being at Baltimore the new Johns Hopkins University, and a hospital had been built under the same endowment. This, after twelve years' work, had now been completed upon modern and admirable lines, and it was decided to sound Osler with the view of his becoming its physician-in-chief. While the university itself, too, was in working order, the medical side of it, in its clinical aspects, was still waiting to be organised, and required a man of exceptional ability. By training and temperament it was just the opportunity of which Osler could take the fullest advantage, and his acceptance of the offer was to become a landmark in the history of medical teaching in the United States. As at Montreal and Philadelphia there were, of course, some initial complaints and jealousies. Osler himself was still under forty, and the three assistants chosen to work under him were all his juniors in age, and none of them was a local man. But their ability was soon beyond doubt. Osler's humanity did the rest. And with the publication, two years later, of his *Principles and Practice of Medicine*, further cavilling at the selectors' judgment became obviously impossible.

To the lay and even the present-day medical mind the significance of this volume is perhaps hard to realise. For not only had Osler succeeded, as somebody said, " in making a scientific treatise literature," but it was the first general text-book to embrace, and re-issue in concise form, the enormous changes wrought in medicine by the discovery of microbic and bacterial infection. To the average practitioner of an older generation it was little short of a new gospel. In the medical schools it was to become the standard book that it has remained ever since. By the year 1905, when Osler came to Oxford, a hundred thousand copies of it had been issued, and only recently, in its revised form, it has been translated into Chinese.

For Osler himself it meant his definite establishment in the foremost ranks of his profession, and a few months later, to his deep and lasting happiness, it was followed by his marriage to Mrs. Gross, the widow of his old friend, and herself an old friend. " I feel very safe," he wrote at the time. And it was because everybody else so instantly felt the same, from the rawest student to the shyest professor, that there was scarcely to be an hour in which his home was not receiving or speeding guests. Every Saturday evening was consecrated to his fourth-year students ; and strictly as he was obliged to map out his time, he was always accessible, if only for a moment, to any of his innumerable friends. And this was equally true of his patients. As one of them was to write after his death, " He made you respect his time, but he also respected yours. A pose or an attempt at a serious chatter about unessentials was intolerable to him. But he was as merciful as he was masterful, and from the poor and the genuinely afflicted he would even have borne being bored." So with his colleagues in the profession— " Three times," said the same lady, " I have seen him, when in consultation, smash the attending physician's diagnosis and turn the entire sick-room the other way about ; but he left the room with his arm round the corrected physician's neck, and they seemed to be having a delightful time."

In the year 1898 he was elected a Fellow of

the Royal Society—three years earlier he had refused the Principalship of McGill University—and on visiting England in 1899 he received honorary degrees both at Edinburgh and Aberdeen. A couple of years afterwards he received a similar honour from Yale, in company, as it happened, with Woodrow Wilson. And in 1904 he was invited to succeed Sir John Burdon Sanderson as Regius Professor of Medicine at Oxford.

From many points of view it was an unprecedented appointment. But the suggestion that it should be made had received powerful support, including that of Sir Herbert Warren, the President of Magdalen, Sir William Broadbent and Sir Victor Horsley. It was true that Osler was a Colonial and that most of his professional life had been spent in the United States ; that, as Dr. Weir Mitchell wrote to him, " the medical school at Johns Hopkins is or was W. Osler." But he had already endeared himself to Oxford as a profound student of medical history and a lover of the classics and the classic quality in all that pertained to the teaching of his art. In his familiarity with the Continental

xxxii

schools he had probably no living English-speaking rival ; and he was also a consultant with an immense experience of actual hospital and private practice.

Had the offer been made to him ten years earlier, it is more than possible that Osler would have refused it. Much of the architecture of his dearly loved school would still have been waiting completion, and there were campaigns to be fought on behalf of municipal sanitation and the new open-air treatment of pulmonary tuberculosis. But he was now fifty-five. There already lay behind him what to most men would have been more than a life's work. And to the book-lover side of him, especially as a medical historian, Oxford made an irresistible appeal. For the third time, therefore, he found himself bidding farewell to a university in mourning, recognising though it did, with legitimate pride, the right of antiquity with which Oxford had approached him. In this, his alma mater McGill, and the University of Pennsylvania also shared ; and it is his farewell address to these universities of his youth that has lent this volume its title.

Of the other three, *Science and Immor-*

tality was given at Harvard, *A Way of Life* to the students of Yale, and *Man's Redemption of Man* to the students of Edinburgh. For all his research, indeed, his myriad journeyings from sick bed to sick bed, it is as the lover and teacher and inspirer of students that Osler will chiefly remain in memory. They are the cloud of witnesses overshadowing all others, and not only students in the sense of youth. When James Mackenzie, for instance, in 1905, was merely an unknown Lancashire doctor, laying the foundations of his work on the heart that was afterwards to carry the world before it, " Osler came to me," he told his friend Dr. McNair Wilson, " when no other of the big physicians would have dreamed of coming." And he might have added that, with the aid of Mackenzie's little girls, he made an apple-pie bed for his fellow-guest.

That was in the year of his coming to Oxford, and though his work there was less spectacular, this was inevitable, since he was now at an old university and not at the birth, as it were, of a new one. But he brought to a medical school that was perhaps somewhat in need of it the invigorating help of a cosmopolitan mind, and it was not very long before his house overlooking the Parks was as thronged with visitors as its fellow had been in Baltimore. For every Canadian and American doctor it became, as a matter of course, an English Mecca, and for most of the Congresses held in Oxford a sort of Anglo-Continental hotel and restaurant. With its growing library, too, of ancient and curious books, it was a happy meeting-ground for bibliophiles of all sorts, and the acknowledged source, amongst other gifts to letters, of one of Kipling's loveliest stories.

For his closing years it was probably just the setting that Osler himself would have chosen, although, with the coming of the War, he was once more faced with every kind of administrative problem. The medical school, of course, had to be kept in being. But he became adviser-in-chief to every Canadian military hospital, and, characteristically enough, when it was all over, the first English spokesman for the stricken Viennese doctors. For this, at the time, he was not uncriticised. But it was wholly consonant with the man, whose " work for others," to quote a brother Regius Professor, " was so incessant and his hospitality so unbounded that one always wondered where and when he had amassed and made use of his learning."

But the War had taken its toll of him. To Lady Osler and himself—he had been made a baronet in 1911—it had meant the loss of their dearly loved and only surviving son. And though this had been borne, outwardly at any rate, with his usual courage and serenity, it was a blow from which, at heart, he had never really recovered before his own death in 1919. Of the faith in which he met this there is evidence in this volume ; and he was probably content that it should have come to him at laſt, surrounded by his books and in his Oxford home and not before his work had been accomplished. From the Bond Head Rectory it had meant a long journey. He had held chairs in four universities. But it had fallen to him to prove, more than any man of his age perhaps, that the life of the spirit has no borders.

THE STUDENT LIFE

" Take therefore no thought for the morrow :
for the morrow shall take thought for the things of
itself."—SERMON ON THE MOUNT.

I

EXCEPT it be a lover, no one is more interesting as an object of study than a student. Shakespeare might have made him a fourth in his immortal group. The lunatic with his fixed idea, the poet with his fine frenzy, the lover with his frantic idolatry, and the student aflame with the desire for knowledge are of " imagination all compact." To an absorbing passion, a whole-souled devotion, must be joined an enduring energy, if the student is to become a devotee of the grey-eyed goddess to whose law his services are bound. Like the quest of the Holy Grail, the quest of Minerva is not for all. For the one, the pure life ; for the other, what Milton calls " a strong propensity of nature." Here again the student often resembles the poet—he is born, not made. While the resultant of two moulding forces, the accidental, external conditions, and the hidden germinal energies, which produce in each one of us national, family, and individual traits, the true student possesses in some measure a divine spark which sets at naught their laws. Like the Snark, he defies definition, but there are three unmistakable signs by which you may recognise the genuine article from a Boojum—an absorbing desire to know the truth, an unswerving steadfastness in its pursuit, and an open, honest heart, free from suspicion, guile, and jealousy.

At the outset do not be worried about this big question—Truth. It is a very simple matter if each one of you starts with the desire to get as much as possible. No human being is constituted to know the truth, the whole truth, and nothing but the truth ; and even the best of men must be content with fragments, with partial glimpses, never the full fruition. In this unsatisfied quest the attitude of mind, the desire, the thirst—a thirst that from the soul must rise ! —the fervent longing, are the be-all and the end-all. What is the student but a lover courting a fickle mistress who ever eludes his grasp ? In this very elusiveness is brought out his second great characteristic—

4

steadfastness of purpose. Unless from the start the limitations incident to our frail human faculties are frankly accepted, nothing but disappointment awaits you. The truth is the best you can get with your best endeavour, the best that the best men accept—with this you must learn to be satisfied, retaining at the same time with due humility an earnest desire for an ever larger portion. Only by keeping the mind plastic and receptive does the student escape perdition. It is not, as Charles Lamb remarks, that some people do not know what to do with truth when it is offered to them, but the tragic fate is to reach, after years of patient search, a condition of mind-blindness in which the truth is not recognised, though it stares you in the face. This can never happen to a man who has followed step by step the growth of a truth, and who knows the painful phases of its evolution. It is one of the great tragedies of life that every truth has to struggle to acceptance against honest but mind-blind students. Harvey knew his contemporaries well, and for twelve successive years demonstrated the circulation of the blood before daring to publish the facts on which the truth was based.* Only steadfastness of purpose and humility enable the student to shift his position to meet the new conditions in which new truths are born, or old ones modified beyond recognition. And, thirdly, the honest heart will keep him in touch with his fellow students, and furnish that sense of comradeship without which he travels an arid waste alone. I say advisedly an honest *heart*—the honest head is prone to be cold and stern, given to judgment, not mercy, and not always able to entertain that true charity which, while it thinketh no evil, is anxious to put the best possible interpretation upon the motives of a fellow worker. It will foster, too, an attitude of generous, friendly rivalry untinged by the green peril, jealousy, that is the best preventive of the growth of a bastard scientific spirit, loving seclusion and working in a lock-and-key laboratory, as timorous of light as is a thief.

You have all become brothers in a great society, not apprentices, since that implies a master, and nothing should be further from

* " These views, as usual, pleased some more, others less; some chid and calumniated me, and laid it to me as a crime that I had dared to depart from the precepts and opinions of all Anatomists."—*De Motu Cordis*, Chap. I.

6

the attitude of the teacher than much that is
meant in that word, used though it be in
another sense, particularly by our French
brethren in a most delightful way, signifying
a bond of intellectual filiation. A fraternal
attitude is not easy to cultivate—the chasm
between the chair and the bench is difficult
to bridge. Two things have helped to put
up a cantilever across the gulf. The successful teacher is no longer on a height, pumping
knowledge at high pressure into passive
receptacles. The new methods have changed
all this. He is no longer *Sir Oracle*, perhaps
unconsciously by his very manner anta-
gonising minds to whose level he cannot
possibly descend, but he is a senior student
anxious to help his juniors. When a simple,
earnest spirit animates a college, there is no
appreciable interval between the teacher and
the taught—both are in the same class, the
one a little more advanced than the other.
So animated, the student feels that he has
joined a family whose honour is his honour,
whose welfare is his own, and whose
interests should be his first consideration.

The hardest conviction to get into the
mind of a beginner is that the education

upon which he is engaged is not a college course, not a medical course, but a life course, for which the work of a few years under teachers is but a preparation. Whether you will falter and fail in the race or whether you will be faithful to the end depends on the training before the start, and on your staying powers, points upon which I need not enlarge. You can all become good students, a few may become great students, and now and again one of you will be found who does easily and well what others cannot do at all, or very badly, which is John Ferriar's excellent definition of a genius.

In the hurry and bustle of a business world, which is the life of this continent, it is not easy to train first-class students. Under present conditions it is hard to get the needful seclusion, on which account it is that our educational market is so full of wayside fruit. I have always been much impressed by the advice of St. Chrysostom: " Depart from the highway and transplant thyself in some enclosed ground, for it is hard for a tree which stands by the wayside to keep her fruit till it be ripe." The dilettante is abroad in the land, the man who is always venturing on tasks for which he is imperfectly equipped, a habit of mind fostered by the multiplicity of subjects in the curriculum ; and while many things are studied, few are studied thoroughly. Men will not take time to get to the heart of a matter. After all, concentration is the price the modern student pays for success. Thoroughness is the most difficult habit to acquire, but it is the pearl of great price, worth all the worry and trouble of the search. The dilettante lives an easy, butter-fly life, knowing nothing of the toil and labour with which the treasures of know-ledge are dug out of the past, or wrung by patient research in the laboratories. Take, for example, the early history of this country —how easy for the student of the one type to get a smattering, even a fairly full acquaint-ance with the events of the French and Spanish settlements. Put an original docu-ment before him, and it might as well be Arabic. What we need is the other type, the man who knows the records, who, with a broad outlook and drilled in what may be called the embryology of history, has yet a powerful vision for the minutiæ of life. It is these kitchen and backstair men who are to be encouraged, the men who know the subject in hand in all possible relationships. Concentration has its drawbacks. It is possible to become so absorbed in the problem of the " enclitic δε," or the structure of the flagella of the Trichomonas, or of the toes of the prehistoric horse, that the student loses the sense of proportion in his work, and even wastes a lifetime in researches which are valueless because not in touch with current knowledge. You remember poor Casaubon, in *Middlemarch*, whose painful scholarship was lost on this account. The best preventive to this is to get denationalised early. The true student is a citizen of the world, the allegiance of whose soul, at any rate, is too precious to be restricted to a single country. The great minds, the great works transcend all limitations of time, of language, and of race, and the scholar can never feel initiated into the company of the elect until he can approach all of life's problems from the cosmopolitan standpoint. I care not in what subject he may work, the full knowledge cannot be reached without drawing on supplies from lands other than his own—French, English, German, American, Japanese, Russian, Italian—there muſt be no discrimination by the loyal ſtudent, who should willingly draw from any and every source with an open mind and a ſtern resolve to render unto all their dues. I care not on what ſtream of knowledge he may embark, follow up its course, and the rivulets that feed it flow from many lands. If the work is to be effeâive he muſt keep in touch with scholars in other countries. How often has it happened that years of precious time have been given to a problem already solved or shown to be insoluble, because of the ignorance of what had been done elsewhere. And it is not only book knowledge and journal knowledge, but a knowledge of men that is needed. The ſtudent will, if possible, see the men in other lands. Travel not only widens the vision and gives certainties in place of vague surmises, but the personal contaâ with foreign workers enables him to appreciate better the failings or successes in his own line of work, perhaps to look with more charitable eyes on the work of some brother whose limitations and opportunities have been more restricted than his own. Or, in contact with a master-mind, he may take fire, and the glow of the enthusiasm may be the inspiration of his life. Concentration must then be associated with large views on the relation of the problem, and a knowledge of its status elsewhere; otherwise it may land him in the slough of a specialism so narrow that it has depth and no breadth, or he may be led to make what he believes to be important discoveries, but which have long been current coin in other lands. It is sad to think that the day of the great polymathic student is at an end; that we may, perhaps, never again see a Scaliger, a Haller, or a Humboldt—men who took the whole field of knowledge for their domain and viewed it as from a pinnacle. And yet a great specialising generalist may arise, who can tell? Some twentieth-century Aristotle may be now tugging at his bottle, as little dreaming as are his parents or his friends of a conquest of the mind, beside which the wonderful victories of the Stagirite will look pale. The value of a really great student to the country is equal to half a dozen grain elevators or a new transcontinental railway.

He is a commodity singularly fickle and variable, and not to be grown to order. So far as his advent is concerned there is no telling when or where he may arise. The conditions seem to be present even under the most unlikely externals. Some of the greatest students this country has produced have come from small villages and country places. It is impossible to predict from a study of the environment, which a " strong propensity of nature," to quote Milton's phrase again, will easily bend or break.

The student must be allowed full freedom in his work, undisturbed by the utilitarian spirit of the Philistine, who cries, *Cui bono ?* and distrusts pure science. The present remarkable position in applied science and in industrial trades of all sorts has been made possible by men who did pioneer work in chemistry, in physics, in biology, and in physiology, without a thought in their researches of any practical application. The members of this higher group of productive students are rarely understood by the common spirits, who appreciate as little their unselfish devotion as their unworldly neglect of the practical side of the problems.

Everywhere now the medical student is
welcomed as an honoured member of the
guild. There was a time, I confess, and it
is within the memory of some of us, when,
like Falstaff, he was given to "taverns and
sack and wine and metheglins, and to drink-
ings and swearings and starings, pribbles and
prabbles "; but all that has changed with the
curriculum, and the " Meds " now roar you
as gently as the " Theologs." On account of
the peculiar character of the subject-matter
of your studies, what I have said upon the
general life and mental attitude of the student
applies with tenfold force to you. Man,
with all his mental and bodily anomalies and
diseases—the machine in order, the machine
in disorder, and the business yours to put it
to rights. Through all the phases of its
career this most complicated mechanism of
this wonderful world will be the subject of
our study and of your care—the naked, new-
born infant, the artless child, the lad and the
lassie just aware of the tree of knowledge
overhead, the strong man in the pride of life,
the woman with the benediction of maternity
on her brow, and the aged, peaceful in the
contemplation of the past. Almost every-

14

thing has been renewed in the science and in the art of medicine, but all through the long centuries there has been no variableness or shadow of change in the essential features of the life which is our contemplation and our care. The sick love-child of Israel's sweet singer, the plague-stricken hopes of the great Athenian statesman, Elpenor bereft of his beloved Artemidora, and "Tully's daughter mourned so tenderly," are not of any age or any race—they are here with us to-day, with the Hamlets, the Ophelias, and the Lears. Amid an eternal heritage of sorrow and suffering our work is laid, and this eternal note of sadness would be insupportable if the daily tragedies were not relieved by the spectacle of the heroism and devotion displayed by the actors. Nothing will sustain you more potently than the power to recognise in your humdrum routine, as perhaps it may be thought, the true poetry of life—the poetry of the commonplace, of the ordinary man, of the plain, toil-worn woman, with their loves and their joys, their sorrows and their griefs. The comedy, too, of life will be spread before you, and nobody laughs more often than the

doctor at the pranks Puck plays upon the
Titanias and the Bottoms among his patients.
The humorous side is really almost as fre-
quently turned towards him as the tragic.
Lift up one hand to heaven and thank your
stars if they have given you the proper sense
to enable you to appreciate the inconceivably
droll situations in which we catch our fellow
creatures. Unhappily, this is one of the free
gifts of the gods, unevenly distributed, not
bestowed on all, or on all in equal portions.
In undue measure it is not without risk, and
in any case in the doctor it is better appreciated by the eye than expressed on the
tongue. Hilarity and good humour, a
breezy cheerfulness, a nature "sloping
toward the southern side," as Lowell has it,
help enormously both in the study and in
the practice of medicine. To many of a
sombre and sour disposition it is hard to
maintain good spirits amid the trials and
tribulations of the day, and yet it is an un-
pardonable mistake to go about among
patients with a long face.

Divide your attentions equally between
books and men. The strength of the student
of books is to sit still—two or three hours at

a stretch—eating the heart out of a subject with pencil and notebook in hand, determined to master the details and intricacies, focussing all your energies on its difficulties. Get accustomed to test all sorts of book problems and statements for yourself, and take as little as possible on trust. The Hunterian " Do not think, but try " attitude of mind is the important one to cultivate. The question came up one day, when discussing the grooves left on the nails after fever, how long it took for the nail to grow out, from root to edge. A majority of the class had no further interest ; a few looked it up in books ; two men marked their nails at the root with nitrate of silver, and a few months later had positive knowledge on the subject. They showed the proper spirit. The little points that come up in your reading try to test for yourselves. With one fundamental difficulty many of you will have to contend from the outset—a lack of proper preparation for really hard study. No one can have watched successive groups of young men pass through the special schools without profoundly regretting the haphazard, fragmentary character of their preliminary education. It does seem too bad that we cannot have a student in his eighteenth year sufficiently grounded in the humanities and in the sciences preliminary to medicine—but this is an educational problem upon which only a Milton or a Locke could discourse with profit. With pertinacity you can overcome the preliminary defects, and, once thoroughly interested, the work in books becomes a pastime. A serious drawback in the student life is the self-consciousness, bred of too close devotion to books. A man gets shy, " dysopic," as old Timothy Bright calls it, and shuns the looks of men, and blushes like a girl.

The strength of a student of men is to travel—to study men, their habits, character, mode of life, their behaviour under varied conditions, their vices, virtues, and peculiarities. Begin with a careful observation of your fellow students and of your teachers ; then, every patient you see is a lesson in much more than the malady from which he suffers. Mix as much as you possibly can with the outside world, and learn its ways. Cultivated systematically, the student societies, the students' union, the gymnasium, and the outside social circle will enable you to conquer the diffidence so apt to go with bookishness and which may prove a very serious drawback in after-life. I cannot too strongly impress upon the earnest and attentive men among you the necessity of overcoming this unfortunate failing in your student days. It is not easy for every one to reach a happy medium, and the distinction between a proper self-confidence and " cheek," particularly in junior students, is not always to be made. The latter is met with chiefly among the student pilgrims who, in travelling down the Delectable Mountains, have gone astray and have passed to the left hand, where lieth the country of Conceit, the country in which you remember the brisk lad Ignorance met Christian.

I wish we could encourage on this continent among our best students the habit of wandering. I do not know that we are quite prepared for it, as there is still great diversity in the curricula, even among the leading schools, but it is undoubtedly a great advantage to study under different teachers, as the mental horizon is widened and the sympathies enlarged. The practice would do much to lessen that narrow " I am of Paul and I am of Apollos " spirit which is hostile to the best interests of the profession.

There is much that I would like to say on the question of work, but I can spare only a few moments for a word or two. Who will venture to settle upon so simple a matter as the best time for work? One will tell us there is no best time; all are equally good; and truly, all times are the same to a man whose soul is absorbed in some great problem. The other day I asked Edward Martin, the well-known story-writer, what time he found best for work. " Not in the evening, and never between meals ! " was his answer, which may appeal to some of my hearers. One works best at night; another, in the morning; a majority of the students of the past favour the latter. Erasmus, the great exemplar, says, " Never work at night; it dulls the brain and hurts the health." One day, going with George Ross through Bedlam, Dr. Savage, at that time the physician in charge, remarked upon two great groups of patients—those who were depressed in the morning and those who were cheerful, and he suggested that the spirits rose and fell with

20

the bodily temperature—those with very low morning temperatures were depressed, and *vice versâ*. This, I believe, expresses a truth which may explain the extraordinary difference in the habits of students in this matter of the time at which the best work can be done. Outside of the asylum there are also the two great types, the student-lark who loves to see the sun rise, who comes to breakfast with a cheerful morning face, never so " fit " as at 6 a.m. We all know the type. What a contrast to the student-owl with his saturnine morning face, thoroughly unhappy, cheated by the wretched breakfast bell of the two best hours of the day for sleep, no appetite, and permeated with an unspeakable hostility to his *vis-à-vis*, whose morning garrulity and good humour are equally offensive. Only gradually, as the day wears on and his temperature rises, does he become endurable to himself and to others. But see him really awake at 10 p.m. while our blithe lark is in hopeless coma over his books, from which it is hard to rouse him sufficiently to get his boots off for bed, our lean owl-friend, Saturn no longer in the ascendant, with bright eyes and cheery face, is ready for four hours of anything you wish—deep study, or

Heart-affluence in discursive talk,

and by 2 a.m. he will undertake to unsphere the spirit of Plato. In neither a virtue, in neither a fault, we must recognise these two types of students, differently constituted, owing possibly—though I have but little evidence for the belief—to thermal peculiarities.

II

In the days of probation the student's life may be lived by each one of you in its fullness and in its joys, but the difficulties arise in the break which follows departure from college and the entrance upon new duties. Much will now depend on the attitude of mind which has been encouraged. If the work has been for your degree, if the diploma has been its sole aim and object, you will rejoice in a freedom from exacting and possibly unpleasant studies, and with your books you will throw away all thoughts of further systematic work. On the other

22

hand, with good habits of observation you
may have got deep enough into the subject
to feel that there is still much to be learned,
and if you have had ground into you the
lesson that the collegiate period is only the
beginning of the student life, there is a hope
that you may enter upon the useful career of
the *student-practitioner.* Five years, at least,
of trial await the man after parting from his
teachers, and entering upon an independent
course—years upon which his future depends, and from which his horoscope may
be cast with certainty. It is all the same
whether he settles in a country village or
goes on with hospital and laboratory work;
whether he takes a prolonged trip abroad;
or whether he settles down in practice, with
a father or a friend—these five waiting years
fix his fate so far as the student life is concerned. Without any strong natural propensity to study, he may feel such a relief
after graduation that the effort to take to
books is beyond his mental strength, and a
weekly journal with an occasional text-book
furnish pabulum enough, at least to keep his
mind hibernating. But ten years later he is
dead mentally, past any possible hope of

galvanizing into life as a student, fit to do a
routine practice, often a capable, resourceful
man, but without any deep convictions, and
probably more interested in stocks or in
horses than in diagnosis or therapeutics.
But this is not always the fate of the student
who finishes his work on Commencement
Day. There are men full of zeal in practice
who give good service to their fellow
creatures, who have not the capacity or the
energy to keep up with the times. While
they have lost interest in science, they are
loyal members of the profession, and appreciate their responsibilities as such. That
fateful first lustrum ruins some of our most
likely material. Nothing is more trying to
the soldier than inaction, to mark time while
the battle is raging all about him; and
waiting for practice is a serious strain under
which many yield. In the cities it is not so
hard to keep up: there is work in the
dispensaries and colleges, and the stimulus
of the medical societies; but in smaller
towns and in the country it takes a strong
man to live through the years of waiting
without some deterioration. I wish the
custom of taking junior men as partners and

assistants would grow on this continent. It has become a necessity, and no man in large general practice can do his work efficiently without skilled help. How incalculably better for the seniors, how beneficial to the patients, how helpful in every way if each one of you, for the first five or ten years, was associated with an older practitioner, doing his night work, his laboratory work, his chores of all sorts. You would, in this way. escape the chilling and killing isolation of the early years, and amid congenial surroundings you could, in time, develop into that flower of our calling—the cultivated general practitioner. May this be the destiny of a large majority of you! Have no higher ambition! You cannot reach any better position in a community ; the family doctor is the man behind the gun, who does our effective work. That his life is hard and exacting ; that he is underpaid and overworked ; that he has but little time for study and less for recreation—these are the blows that may give finer temper to his steel, and bring out the nobler elements in his character. What lot or portion has the general practitioner in the student life ? Not,

25

perhaps, the fruitful heritage of Judah or Benjamin, but he may make of it the goodly portion of Ephraim. A man with powers of observation, well trained in the wards, and with the strong natural propensity to which I have so often referred, may live the ideal student life, and even reach the higher levels of scholarship. Adams, of Banchory (a little Aberdeenshire village), was not only a good practitioner and a skilful operator, but he was an excellent naturalist. This is by no means an unusual or remarkable combination, but Adams became, in addition, one of the great scholars of the profession. He had a perfect passion for the classics, and amid a very exacting practice found time to read " almost every Greek work which has come down to us from antiquity, except the ecclesiastical writers." He translated the works of Paulus Aegineta, the works of Hippocrates, and the works of Aretaeus, all of which are in the Sydenham Society's publications, monuments of the patient skill and erudition of a Scottish village doctor, an incentive to every one of us to make better use of our precious time.

26

Given the sacred hunger and proper preliminary training, the student-practitioner requires at least three things with which to stimulate and maintain his education, a notebook, a library, and a quinquennial braindusting. I wish I had time to speak of the value of note-taking. You can do nothing as a student in practice without it. Carry a small note-book which will fit into your waistcoat pocket, and never ask a new patient a question without note-book and pencil in hand. After the examination of a pneumonia case two minutes will suffice to record the essentials in the daily progress. Routine and system, when once made a habit, facilitate work, and the busier you are the more time you will have to make observations after examining a patient. Jot a comment at the end of the notes : " clear case," " case illustrating obscurity of symptoms," " error in diagnosis," etc. The . making of observations may become the exercise of a jackdaw trick, like the craze which so many of us have to collect articles of all sorts. The study of the cases, the relation they bear to each other and to the cases in literature—here comes in the diffi-

27

culty. Begin early to make a threefold category—clear cases, doubtful cases, mistakes. And learn to play the game fair, no self-deception, no shrinking from the truth; mercy and consideration for the other man, but none for yourself, upon whom you have to keep an incessant watch. You remember Lincoln's famous *mot* about the impossibility of fooling all of the people all the time. It does not hold good for the individual who can fool himself to his heart's content all of the time. If necessary, be cruel; use the knife and the cautery to cure the intumescence and moral necrosis which you will feel in the posterior parietal region, in Gall and Spurzheim's centre of self-esteem, where you will find a sore spot after you have made a mistake in diagnosis. It is only by getting your cases grouped in this way that you can make any real progress in your post-collegiate education; only in this way can you gain wisdom with experience. It is a common error to think that the more a doctor sees the greater his experience and the more he knows. No one ever drew a more skilful distinction than Cowper in his oft-quoted lines, which I am never tired of repeating in a medical audience :

> Knowledge and wisdom, far from being one,
> Have oft-times no connexion. Knowledge dwells
> In heads replete with thoughts of other men ;
> Wisdom in minds attentive to their own.
> Knowledge is proud that he has learned so much ;
> Wisdom is humble that he knows no more.

What we call sense or wisdom is knowledge, ready for use, made effective, and bears the same relation to knowledge itself that bread does to wheat. The full knowledge of the parts of a steam engine and the theory of its action may be possessed by a man who could not be trusted to pull the lever to its throttle. It is only by collecting data and using them that you can get sense. One of the most delightful sayings of antiquity is the remark of Heraclitus upon his predecessors—that they had much knowledge but no sense—which indicates that the noble old Ephesian had a keen appreciation of their difference ; and the distinction, too, is well drawn by Tennyson in the oft-quoted line :

> Knowledge comes but wisdom lingers.

Of the three well-stocked rooms which it

29

should be the ambition of every young
doctor to have in his house, the library, the
laboratory, and the nursery—books, balances
and bairns—as he may not achieve all three,
I would urge him to start at any rate with
the books and the balances. A good
weekly and a good monthly journal to begin
with, and read them. Then, for a systematic course of study, supplement your
college text-books with the larger systems—
Allbutt or Nothnagel—a system of surgery
and, as your practice increases, make a habit
of buying a few special monographs every
year. Read with two objects : first, to
acquaint yourself with the current knowledge on the subject and the steps by which
it has been reached ; and secondly, and more
important, read to understand and analyse
your cases. To this line of work we should
direct the attention of the student before he
leaves the medical school, pointing in specific
cases just where the best articles are to be
found, sending him to the Index Catalogue—
that marvellous storehouse, every page of
which is interesting and the very titles in-
structive. Early learn to appreciate the
differences between the descriptions of disease

30

and the manifestations of that disease in an individual—the difference between the composite portrait and one of the component pictures. By exercise of a little judgment you can collect at moderate cost a good working library. Try, in the waiting years, to get a clear idea of the history of medicine. Read Foster's *Lectures on the History of Physiology* and Baas's *History of Medicine.* Get the " Masters of Medicine " Series, and subscribe to the *Library and Historical Journal.*

Every day do some reading or work apart from your profession. I fully realise, no one more so, how absorbing is the profession of medicine ; how applicable to it is what Michelangelo says : " There are sciences which demand the whole of a man, without leaving the least portion of his spirit free for other distractions " ; but you will be a better man and not a worse practitioner for an avocation. I care not what it may be ; gardening or farming, literature or history or bibliography, any one of which will bring you into contact with books. (I wish that time permitted me to speak of the other two rooms which are really of equal importance with the library, but which are more difficult

to equip, though of co-ordinate value in the
education of the head, the heart, and the
hand.) The third essential for the practitioner as a student is the quinquennial braindusting, and this will often seem to him the
hardest task to carry out. Every fifth year,
back to the hospital, back to the laboratory,
for renovation, rehabilitation, rejuvenation,
reintegration, resuscitation, etc. Do not
forget to take the note-books with you, or the
sheets, in three separate bundles, to work
over. From the very start begin to save
for the trip. Deny yourself all luxuries for
it ; shut up the room you meant for the
nursery—have the definite determination to
get your education thoroughly well started ;
if you are successful you may, perhaps, have
enough saved at the end of three years to
spend six weeks in special study ; or in five
years you may be able to spend six months.
Hearken not to the voice of old " Dr.
Hayseed," who tells you it will ruin your
prospects, and that he " never heard of such
a thing " as a young man, not yet five years
in practice, taking three months' holiday.
To him it seems preposterous. Watch him
wince when you say it is a speculation in the

only gold mine in which the physician should invest—*Grey Cortex* ! What about the wife and babies, if you have them ? Leave them ! Heavy as are your responsibilities to those nearest and dearest, they are outweighed by the responsibilities to yourself, to the profession, and to the public. Like Isaphaena, the story of whose husband—ardent, earnest soul, peace to his ashes !—I have told in the little sketch of *An Alabama Student,** your wife will be glad to bear her share in the sacrifice you make.

With good health and good habits the end of the second lustrum should find you thoroughly established—all three rooms well furnished, a good stable, a good garden, no mining stock, but a life insurance, and perhaps a mortgage or two on neighbouring farms. Year by year you have dealt honestly with yourself ; you have put faithfully the notes of each case into their proper places, and you will be gratified to find that, though the doubtful cases and mistakes still make a rather formidable pile, it has grown relatively smaller. You literally " own " the

* *An Alabama Student and other Biographical Essays*, Oxford, 1908 ; reprinted 1926.

countryside, as the expression is. All the serious and dubious cases come to you, and you have been so honest in the frank acknowledgment of your own mistakes, and so charitable in the contemplation of theirs, that neighbouring doctors, old and young, are glad to seek your advice. The work, which has been very heavy, is now lightened by a good assistant, one of your own students, who becomes in a year or so your partner. This is not an overdrawn picture, and it is one which may be seen in many places except, I am sorry to say, in the particular as to the partner. This is the type of man we need in the country districts and the smaller towns. He is not a whit too good to look after the sick, not a whit too highly educated—impossible! And with an optimistic temperament and a good digestion he is the very best product of our profession, and may do more to stop quackery and humbuggery, inside and out-side of the ranks, than could a dozen prosecuting county attorneys. Nay, more! such a doctor may be a daily benediction in the community—a strong, sensible, whole-souled man, often living a life of great self-

34

denial, and always of tender sympathy,
worried neither by the vagaries of the well
nor by the testy waywardness of the sick,
and to him, if to any, may come (even when
he knows it not) the true spiritual blessing
—that " blessing which maketh rich and
addeth no sorrow."

The danger in such a man's life comes
with prosperity. He is safe in the hard-
working day, when he is climbing the hill,
but once success is reached, with it come the
temptations to which many succumb. Politics
have been the ruin of many country doctors,
and often of the very best, of just such a
good fellow as he of whom I have been
speaking. He is popular; he has a little
money; and he, if anybody, can save the
seat for the party! When the committee
leaves you, take the offer under consideration, and if in the ten or twelve years you
have kept on intimate terms with those
friends of your student days, Montaigne and
Plutarch, you will know what answer to
return. If you live in a large town, resist
the temptation to open a sanatorium. It is
not the work for a general practitioner, and
there are risks that you may sacrifice your

independence and much else besides. And, thirdly, resist the temptation to move into a larger place. In a good agricultural district, or in a small town, if you handle your resources aright, taking good care of your education, of your habits, and of your money, and devoting part of your energies to the support of the societies, etc., you may reach a position in the community of which any man may be proud. There are country practitioners among my friends with whom I would rather change places than with any in our ranks, men whose stability of character and devotion to duty make one proud of the profession.

Curiously enough, the student-practitioner may find studiousness to be a stumbling-block in his career. A bookish man may never succeed; deep-versed in books, he may not be able to use his knowledge to practical effect; or, more likely, his failure is not because he has studied books much, but because he has not studied men more. He has never got over that shyness, that diffidence, against which I have warned you. I have known instances in which this malady was incurable; in others I have known a

36

cure effected not by the public, but by the man's professional brethren, who, appreciating his work, have insisted upon utilising his mental treasures. It is very hard to carry student habits into a large city practice; only zeal, a fiery passion, keeps the flame alive, smothered as it is so apt to be by the dust and ashes of the daily routine. A man may be a good student who reads only the book of Nature. Such a one * I remember in the early days of my residence in Montreal —a man whose devotion to patients and whose kindness and skill quickly brought him an enormous practice. Reading in his carriage and by lamplight at Lucina's bedside, he was able to keep well informed; but he had an insatiable desire to know the true inwardness of a disease, and it was in this way I came into contact with him. Hard pushed day and night, yet he was never too busy to spend a couple of hours with me searching for data which had not been forthcoming during life, or helping to unravel the mysteries of a new disease, such as pernicious anæmia.

* The late John Bell.

III

The *student-specialist* has to walk warily, as
with two advantages there are two great
dangers against which he has constantly to
be on guard. In the bewildering complexity
of modern medicine it is a relief to limit the
work of a life to a comparatively narrow
field which can be thoroughly tilled. To
many men there is a feeling of great satisfaction in the mastery of a small department,
particularly one in which technical skill is
required. How much we have benefited
from this concentration of effort in derma-
tology, laryngology, ophthalmology, and in
gynæcology! Then, as a rule, the specialist
is a free man, with leisure or, at any rate,
with some leisure; not the slave of the
public, with the incessant demands upon
him of the general practitioner. He may live
a more rational life, and has time to cultivate
his mind, and he is able to devote himself to
public interests and to the welfare of his
professional brethren, on whose suffrages
he so largely depends. How much we are
indebted in the larger cities to the disin-
terested labours of this favoured class the

records of our libraries and medical societies bear witness. The dangers do not come to the strong man in a speciality, but to the weak brother who seeks in it an easier field in which specious garrulity and mechanical dexterity may take the place of solid knowledge. All goes well when the man is larger than his speciality and controls it, but when the speciality runs away with the man there is disaster, and a topsy-turvy condition which, in every branch, has done incalculable injury. Next to the danger from small men is the serious risk of the loss of perspective in prolonged and concentrated effort in a narrow field. Against this there is but one safeguard—the cultivation of the sciences upon which the speciality is based. The student-specialist may have a wide vision— no student wider—if he gets away from the mechanical side of the art, and keeps in touch with the physiology and pathology upon which his art depends. More than any other of us, he needs the lessons of the laboratory, and wide contact with men in other departments may serve to correct the inevitable tendency to a narrow and perverted vision, in which the life of the ant-hill is mistaken for the world at large.

Of the *student-teacher* every faculty affords examples in varying degrees. It goes without saying that no man can teach successfully who is not at the same time a student. Routine, killing routine, saps the vitality of many who start with high aims, and who, for years, strive with all their energies against the degeneration which it is so prone to entail. In the smaller schools isolation, the absence of congenial spirits working at the same subject, favours stagnation, and after a few years the fires of early enthusiasm no longer glow in the perfunctory lectures. In many teachers the ever-increasing demands of practice leave less and less time for study, and a first-class man may lose touch with his subject through no fault of his own, but through an entanglement in outside affairs which he deeply regrets yet cannot control. To his five natural senses the student-teacher must add two more—the sense of responsibility and the sense of proportion. Most of us start with a highly developed sense of the importance of the work, and with a desire to live up to the

40

responsibilities entrusted to us. Punctuality, the class first, always and at all times; the best that a man has in him, nothing less; the best the profession has on the subject, nothing less; fresh energies and enthusiasm in dealing with dry details; animated, unselfish devotion to all alike; tender consideration for his assistants—these are some of the fruits of a keen sense of responsibility in a good teacher. The sense of proportion is not so easy to acquire, and much depends on the training and on the natural disposition. There are men who never possess it; to others it seems to come naturally. In the most careful ones it needs constant cultivation—*nothing over-much* should be the motto of every teacher. In my early days I came under the influence of an ideal student-teacher, the late Palmer Howard, of Montreal. If you ask what manner of man he was, read Matthew Arnold's noble tribute to his father in his well-known poem, *Rugby Chapel*. When young, Dr. Howard had chosen a path—" path to a clear-purposed goal," and he pursued it with unswerving devotion. With him the study and the teaching of medicine were an absorbing passion,

41

the ardour of which neither the incessant
and ever-increasing demands upon his time
nor the growing years could quench. When
I first, as a senior student, came into intimate
contact with him in the summer of 1871, the
problem of tuberculosis was under discussion, stirred up by the epoch-making work
of Villemin and the radical views of Nie-
meyer. Every lung lesion at the Montreal
General Hospital had to be shown to him,
and I got my first-hand introduction to
Laennec, to Graves, and to Stokes, and
became familiar with their works. No
matter what the hour, and it usually was
after 10 p.m., I was welcome with my bag,
and if Wilks and Moxon, Virchow, or
Rokitanski gave us no help, there were the
Transactions of the Pathological Society and
the big *Dictionnaire* of Dechambre. An ideal
teacher because a student, ever alert to the
new problems, an indomitable energy enabled him in the midst of an exacting practice
to maintain an ardent enthusiasm, still to
keep bright the fires which he had lighted in
his youth. Since those days I have seen
many teachers, and I have had many colleagues, but I have never known one in

42

whom was more happily combined a stern sense of duty with the mental freshness of youth.

But as I speak, from out the memory of the past there rises before me a shadowy group, a long line of students whom I have taught and loved, and who have died prematurely—mentally, morally, or bodily. To the successful we are willing and anxious to bring the tribute of praise, but none so poor to give recognition to the failures. From one cause or another, perhaps because when not absorbed in the present, my thoughts are chiefly in the past, I have cherished the memory of many young men whom I have loved and lost. *Io victis :* let us sometimes sing of the vanquished. Let us sometimes think of those who have fallen in the battle of life, who have striven and failed, who have failed even without the strife. How many have I lost from the student band by mental death, and from so many causes—some stillborn from college, others dead within the first year of infantile marasmus, while mental rickets, teething, tabes, and fits have carried off many of the most promising minds ! Due to improper feeding within the

first five fateful years, scurvy and rickets
head the mental mortality bills of students.
To the teacher-nurse it is a sore disappointment to find at the end of ten years so few
minds with the full stature, of which the
early days gave promise. Still, so wide-
spread is mental death that we scarcely comment upon it in our friends. The real
tragedy is the moral death which, in different
forms, overtakes so many good fellows
who fall away from the pure, honourable,
and righteous service of Minerva into the
idolatry of Bacchus, of Venus, or of Circe.
Against the background of the past these
tragedies stand out, lurid and dark, and as
the names and faces of my old boys recur
(some of them my special pride), I shudder
to think of the blighted hopes and wrecked
lives, and I force my memory back to those
happy days when they were as you are now,
joyous and free from care, and I think of
them on the benches, in the laboratories, and
in the wards—and there I leave them. Less
painful to dwell upon, though associated
with a more poignant grief, is the fate of
those whom physical death has snatched
away in the bud or blossom of the student

44

life. These are among the tender memories of the teacher's life, of which he does not often care to speak, feeling with Longfellow that the surest pledge of their remembrance is " the silent homage of thoughts unspoken." As I look back it seems now as if the best of us had died, that the brightest and the keenest had been taken and the more commonplace among us had been spared. An old mother, a devoted sister, a loving brother, in some cases a broken-hearted wife, still pay the tribute of tears for the untimely ending of their high hopes, and in loving remembrance I would mingle mine with theirs. What a loss to our profession have been the deaths of such true disciples as Zimmerman, of Toronto; of Jack Cline and of R. L. MacDonnell, of Montreal; of Fred Packard and of Kirkbride, of Philadelphia; of Livingood, of Lazear, of Oppenheimer, and of Oechsner, in Baltimore—cut off with their leaves still in the green, to the inconsolable grief of their friends!

To each one of you the practice of medicine will be very much as you make it—to one a worry, a care, a perpetual annoyance; to another, a daily joy and a life of as much

45

happiness and usefulness as can well fall to the lot of man. In the student spirit you can best fulfil the high mission of our noble calling—in his *humility*, conscious of weakness, while seeking strength; in his *confidence*, knowing the power, while recognising the limitations of his art; in his *pride* in the glorious heritage from which the greatest gifts to man have been derived, and in his sure and certain hope that the future holds for us still richer blessings than the past.

MAN'S REDEMPTION OF MAN

And a man shall be as an hiding-place from the wind, and a covert from the tempest; as rivers of water in a dry place; as the shadow of a great rock in a weary land.

And the voice of weeping shall be no more heard in her, nor the voice of crying. There shall be no more thence an infant of days, nor an old man that hath not filled his days.

(Isaiah.)

To man there has been published a triple gospel—of his soul, of his goods, of his body. Growing with his growth, preached and professed in a hundred different ways in various ages of the world, these gospels represent the unceasing purpose of his widening thoughts.

The gospel of his relation to the powers unseen has brought sometimes hope, too often despair. In a wide outlook on the immediate and remote effects of the attempts to establish this relation, one event discredits the great counsel of Confucius (who realised what a heavy yoke religion might be) to keep aloof from spiritual beings. Surviving the accretions of twenty centuries, the life and immortality brought to light by the gospel of Christ remain the earnest desire of the best portion of the race.

The gospel of his goods—of man's relation to his fellow men, is written in blood on every page of history. Quietly and slowly the righteousness that exalteth a nation, the principles of eternal justice, have won acquiescence, at any rate in theory, though as nations and individuals we are still far from carrying them into practice.

And the third gospel, the gospel of his body, which brings man into relation with Nature—a true *evangelion*, the glad tidings of a conquest beside which all others sink into insignificance—is the final conquest of Nature, out of which has come man's redemption of man, the subject to which I am desirous of directing your attention.

In the struggle for existence in which all life is engaged, disease and pain loom large as fundamental facts. The whole creation groaneth and travaileth, and so red in tooth and claw with ravin is Nature, that, it is said, no animal in a wild state dies a natural death. The history of man is the story of a great martyrdom—plague, pestilence and famine, battle and murder, crimes unspeakable, tortures inconceivable; and the inhumanity of man to man has even outdone what appear to be atrocities in Nature. In the *Grammar of Assent* (Chap. X.) Cardinal Newman has an interesting paragraph on this great mystery of the physical world. Speaking of the amount of suffering bodily and mental which is our lot and heritage, he says: " Not only is the Creator far off, but some being of malignant nature seems to have got hold of us, and to be making us his sport. Let us say that there are a thousand millions of men on the earth at this time; who can weigh and measure the aggregate of pain which this one generation has endured, and will endure from birth to death? Then add to this all the pain which has fallen and will fall upon our race through generations past and to come. Is there not then some great gulf fixed between us and the good God?"

Dwelling too exclusively on this aspect of life, who does not echo the wish of Euripides: "Not to be born is the best, and next to die as soon as possible"?

Some of you may remember Edwin Markham's poem, " The Man with the Hoe," based on Millet's famous picture.

Bowed by the weight of centuries he leans
Upon his hoe and gazes on the ground,
The emptiness of ages in his face,
And on his back the burden of the world.
Who made him dead to rapture and despair,
A thing that grieves not and that never hopes,
Stolid and stunned, a brother to the ox?

It is a world-old tale, this of the trembling heart, the failing eyes, the desponding mind of the natural man. "And thy life shall hang in doubt before thee; and thou shalt fear day and night, and shalt have none assurance of thy life: In the morning thou shalt say, Would God it were even! and at even thou shalt say, Would God it were morning! for the fear of thine heart wherewith thou shalt fear, and for the sight of thine eyes which thou shalt see" (Deut. xxviii.).

The condition of Hopeful and Christian put by Giant Despair into "a very dark dungeon, nasty and stinking to their spirits," and beaten with stripes, and made to feel that the bitterness of death was as nothing to the bitterness of life, illustrates in allegory the state of man for countless centuries. In darkness and in the shadow of death he lay helpless, singing like the prisoners vain hymns of hope, and praying vain prayers of patience, yet having all the while in his bosom, like Christian, a key called Promise, capable of unlocking the doors of his dungeon. Groping between what Sir Thomas Browne so finely calls "the night of our fore-being" and the unknown future, the dark before and after, he at laſt came to himself, and with the help of this key unlocked the myſteries of Nature, and found a way of physical salvation.

Man's redemption of man is the great triumph of Greek thought. The tap-root of modern science sinks deep in Greek soil, the aſtounding fertility of which is one of the outſtanding faƈts of hiſtory. As Sir Henry Maine says : " To one small people . . . it was given to create the principle of progress. That people was the Greek. Except the blind forces of Nature nothing moves in this world which is not Greek in its origin." Though not always recognised, the controlling principles of our art, literature and philosophy, as well as thosc of science, are Hellenic. We ſtill think in certain levels only with the help of Plato, and there is not a leƈture room of this university * in which the trained ear may not catch echoes of the Lyceum. In the introduƈtory chapter of his *Rise of the Greek Epic*, Professor Murray dwells on the keen desire of the Greeks to make life a better thing than it is, and to help in the service of man, a thought

* *Edinburgh.*

53

that pervades Greek life like an aroma.
From Homer to Lucian there is one refrain
—the pride in the body as a whole ; and in
the strong conviction that " our soul in its
rose-mesh " is quite as much helped by
flesh as flesh is by soul, the Greek sang his
song, " For pleasant is this flesh." The
beautiful soul harmonising with a beautiful
body is as much the glorious ideal of Plato
as it is the end of the education of Aristotle.
What a splendid picture in Book III. of the
Republic, of the day when " our youth will
dwell in a land of health, amid fair sights and
sounds and receive the good in everything ;
and beauty, the effluence of fair works, shall
flow into the eye and ear like a health-giving
breeze from a purer region, and insensibly
draw the soul from earliest years into likeness
and sympathy with the beauty of reason." The
glory of this zeal for the enrichment of the
present life was revealed to the Greeks as
to no other people, but in respect to care for
the body of the common man, we have only
seen its fulfilment in our own day, but as a
direct result of methods of research initiated
by them.

Philosophy, as Plato tells us, begins with

wonder; and, staring open-eyed at the
starry heavens on the plains of Mesopo-
tamia, man took a first step in the careful
observation of Nature, which carried him a
long way in his career. But he was very
slow to learn the second step—how to inter-
rogate Nature, to search out her secrets, as
Harvey puts it, by way of experiment. The
Chaldeans, who invented gnomons, and predicted eclipses, made a good beginning.
The Greeks did not get much beyond
trained observation, though Pythagoras
made one fundamental experiment when he
determined the dependence of the pitch of
sound on the length of the vibrating cord.
So far did unaided observation and brilliant
generalisation carry Greek thinkers, that
there is scarcely a modern discovery which
by anticipation cannot be found in their
writings. Indeed one is staggered at their
grasp of great principles. Man can do a great
deal by observation and thinking, but with
them alone he cannot unravel the mysteries
of Nature. Had it been possible, the Greeks
would have done it; and could Plato and
Aristotle have grasped the value of experiment in the progress of human knowledge,

the course of European history might have been very different.

This organon was absent, and even in the art of medicine Hippocrates with all his genius did not get beyond highly trained observation, and a conception of disease as a process of Nature. The great Pergamite, Galen, did indeed realise that the bare fact was only preliminary to the scientific study of disease by experiment, and to the collecting of data, from which principles and laws could be derived. On the dark horizon of the ancient world shone the brightness of the Grecian dawn so clearly that the emancipated mind had an open way. Then something happened—how, who can tell ? The light failed or flickered almost to extinction : Greece died into a mediævalism that for centuries enthralled man in chains, the weary length of which still hampers his progress. The revival of learning awakened at first a suspicion and then a conviction that salvation lay in a return to the old Greek fathers who had set man's feet in the right path, and so it came about that in the study of chemistry, and in the inventions of Copernicus, Kepler and Galileo, modern science took its origin. The growth of the experimental method changed the outlook of mankind, and led directly in the development of the physical and biological sciences by which the modern world has been transformed.

A slow, painful progress, through three centuries, science crept on from point to point, with many mistakes and many failures, a progress often marked and flecked with the stains of human effort, but all the same the most revolutionary and far-reaching advance ever made by man's intellect. We are too close to the events to appreciate fully the changes which it has wrought in man's relation to the world; and the marvellous thing is that the most important of these changes have been effected within the memory of those living. Three stand out as of the first importance.

My generation was brought up in the belief that " Man was in the original state a very noble and exalted creature, being placed as the head and lord of this world, having all the creatures in subjection to him. The powers and operations of his mind were extensive, capacious and perfect "—to quote the words of one of my old Sunday-school

57

lessons. It is not too much to say that Charles Darwin has so turned man right-about-face that, no longer looking back with regret upon a Paradise Lost, he feels already within the gates of a Paradise Regained.

Secondly, Chemistry and Physics have at last given him control of the four elements, and he has harnessed the forces of Nature. As usual Kipling touches the very heart of the matter in his poem on "The Four Angels," who in succession offered to Adam fire, air, earth and water. Happy in the garden, watching the apple tree in bud, in leaf, in blossom and in fruit, he had no use for them; but when the apple tree was cut down, and he had to work outside of Eden wall,—then—

> out of black disaster
> He arose to be the master
> Of Earth and Water, Air and Fire.

And this mastery, won in our day, has made the man with the hoe look up.

But the third and greatest glory is that the leaves of the tree of science have availed for the healing of the nations. Measure as we may the progress of the world—intellectually in the growth and spread of education, materially in the application to life of all mechanical appliances, and morally in a higher standard of ethics between nation and nation, and between individuals—there is no one measure which can compare with the decrease of disease and suffering in man, woman and child. The Psalmist will have it that no man may redeem his brother, but this redemption of his body has been bought at a price of the lives of those who have sought out Nature's processes by study and experiment. Silent workers, often unknown and neglected by their generation, these men have kept alive the fires on the altars of science, and have so opened the doors of knowledge that we now know the laws of health and disease. Time will only permit me to refer to a few of the more important of the measures of man's physical redemption.

Within the lifetime of some of us a strange and wonderful thing happened on the earth—something of which no prophet foretold, of which no seer dreamt, nor is it among the beatitudes of Christ Himself; only St. John seems to have had an inkling of it in that splendid chapter in which he describes the new heaven and the new earth, when the former things should pass away, when all tears should be wiped away, and there should be no more crying nor sorrow. On October 16, 1846, in the amphitheatre of the Massachusetts General Hospital, Boston, a new Prometheus gave a gift as rich as that of fire, the greatest single gift ever made to suffering humanity. The prophecy was fulfilled—*neither shall there be any more pain;* a mystery of the ages had been solved by a daring experiment by man on man in the introduction of anæsthesia. As Weir Mitchell sings in his poem, "The Death of Pain "—

> Whatever triumphs still shall hold the mind,
> Whatever gifts shall yet enrich mankind,
> Ah! here, no hour shall strike through all the
>   years,
> No hour so sweet as when hope, doubt and fears,
> 'Mid deepening silence watched one eager brain
> With Godlike will decree the Death of Pain.

At a stroke the curse of Eve was removed, that multiplied sorrow of sorrows, representing in all ages the very apotheosis of pain. The knife has been robbed of its terrors, and the hospitals are no longer the scenes of those appalling tragedies that made the stoutest quail. To-day we take for granted the silence of the operating-room, but to reach this Elysium we had to travel the slow road of laborious research, which gave us first the chemical agents ; and then brave hearts had to risk reputation, and even life itself in experiments, the issue of which was for long doubtful.

More widespread in its benediction, as embracing all races and all classes of society, is the relief of suffering, and the prevention of disease through the growth of modern sanitary science in which has been fought out the greatest victory in history. I can only refer to three subjects which illustrate and lead up to the question which is in the minds of all of us to-day.

You have in Scotland the merit of the practical introduction of a method which has revolutionised the treatment of wounds, and changed the whole aspect of modern surgery. I am old enough to have been a dresser in a large general hospital in the pre-Listerian days, when it was the rule for wounds to suppurate, and when cases of severe pyæmia and septicæmia were so

61

common that surgeons dreaded to make even a simple amputation. In the wards of the Edinburgh Royal Infirmary and of the Glasgow Royal Infirmary, Lord Lister's experimental work on the healing of wounds led to results of the deepest moment to every individual subject to an accident, or who has to submit to an operation. It is not simply that the prospect of recovery is enormously enhanced, but Listerian surgery has diminished suffering to an extraordinary degree. In the old days every wound which suppurated had to be dressed, and there was the daily distress and pain, felt particularly by young children. Now, even after operations of the first magnitude, the wound may have but a single dressing, and the after-pain is reduced to a minimum. How well the older ones of us realise that anæsthetics and asepsis between them have wrought a complete revolution in hospital life. I asked the Superintendent of Nurses at the Royal Infirmary to let me know how many patients last night in the wards had actual suffering, and she has sent word that about one in eight had pain, not all of them acute pain.

But man's redemption of man is nowhere

so well known as in the abolition and prevention of the group of diseases which we
speak of as the fevers, or the acute infections.
This is the glory of the science of medicine,
and nowhere in the world have its lessons
been so thoroughly carried out as in this
country. It is too old a story to re-tell in
detail, but I may remind you that in this
city within fifty years there has been an
annual saving of from four to five thousand
lives, by measures which have directly prevented and limited the spread of infectious
diseases. The man is still alive, Sir Henry
Littlejohn, who made the first sanitary sur-
vey of the city. When one reads the account
of the condition of the densely crowded
districts on the south side of the High Street,
one is not surprised that the rate of mortality
was 40 and over per thousand. That you
now enjoy one of the lowest death rates in
Europe—15·3 per thousand for last year—
is due to the thoroughness with which
measures of recognised efficiency have been
carried out. When we learn that last year
there were no deaths from smallpox, not
one from typhus, and only 21 from fevers of
the zymotic group, it is scarcely credible

that all this has been brought about within the memory of living men. It is not too much to say that the abolition of smallpox, typhus and typhoid fevers has changed the character of the medical practice in our hospitals. In this country typhoid fever is in its last ditch, and though a more subtle and difficult enemy to conquer than typhus, we may confidently hope that before long it will be as rare.

Here I would like to say a word or two upon one of the most terrible of all acute infections, the one of which we first learned the control through the work of Jenner. A great deal of literature has been distributed casting discredit upon the value of vaccination in the prevention of smallpox. I do not see how any one who has gone through epidemics as I have, or who is familiar with the history of the subject, and who has any capacity left for clear judgment, can doubt its value. Some months ago I was twitted by the Editor of the *Journal of the Anti-Vaccination League* for maintaining a curious silence on the subject. I would like to issue a Mount Carmel - like challenge to any ten unvaccinated priests of Baal. I will

64

take ten selected vaccinated persons, and help in the next severe epidemic, with ten selected unvaccinated persons (if available !). I should choose three members of Parliament, three anti-vaccination doctors, if they could be found, and four anti-vaccination propagandists. And I will make this promise—neither to jeer nor to jibe when they catch the disease, but to look after them as brothers ; and for the three or four who are certain to die I will try to arrange the funerals with all the pomp and ceremony of an anti-vaccination demonstration.

A blundering art until thirty or forty years ago, preventive medicine was made a science by the discovery of the causes of many of the serious epidemic diseases. To any one of you who wishes to know this side of science, what it is, what it has done, what it may do, let me commend Radot's *Life of Pasteur*, which reads like a fairy tale. It is more particularly in connection with the great plagues of the world that man's redemption of man may be in the future effected ; I say in the future because we have only touched the fringe of the subject. How little do we appreciate what even a generation has done. The man is only just dead, Robert Koch, who gave to his fellowmen the control of cholera. Read the history of yellow fever in Havana and in Brazil if you wish to get an idea of the powers of experimental medicine ; there is nothing to match it in the history of human achievement. Before our eyes to-day the most striking experiment ever made in sanitation is in progress. The digging of the Panama Canal was acknowledged to be a question of the health of the workers. For four centures the Isthmus had been a white man's grave, and during the French control of the Canal the mortality once reached the appalling figure of 170 per thousand. Even under the most favourable circumstances it was extraordinarily high. Month by month I get the *Reports* which form by far the most interesting sanitary reading of the present day. Of more than 54,000 employés (about 13,000 of whom are white), the death rate per thousand for the month of March was 8·91, a lower percentage, I believe, than any city in the United States. It has been brought about in great part by researches into the life history of the parasite which produces

66

malaria, and by the effectual measures taken for its destruction. Here again is a chapter in human achievement for which it would be hard to find a parallel. But let us not forget that these are but illustrations of wide-spread possibilities of organisation on modern lines. These are sanitary blessings. To make them available in the Tropics is the heaviest burden of the white man ; how heavy you may know from the startling figures which have just been issued from British India. Exclusive of the native states for the year 1908, the total deaths from fever and cholera exceeded 5,000,000, out of a population of 226,000,000. The bright spot in the picture is the diminution of the mortality from plague—not fewer than a million fatal cases as compared with 1907.

These are brief indications of the lines along which effective progress is being made in man's redemption by man. And all this has a direct bearing upon the disease, the fight against which brings us together. Tuberculosis is one of the great infections of the world, and it has been one of the triumphs of our generation to determine its cause. With the improvement of sanitation

there has been a reduction in its mortality,
amounting since 1850 to above 40 per cent.
But it still remains the most formidable
single foe, killing a larger number of people
than any other disease—some 60,000 in
Great Britain and Ireland in 1908, and 589
of this city. Practically between 10 and 11
per cent. of all deaths are due to it. A plain
proposition is before the people. We know
the disease—how it is caused, how it is
spread, how it should be prevented, how in
suitable cases it may be cured. How to
make this knowledge effective is the prime
reason of this conference. It is a campaign
for the public ; past history shows that it is
a campaign of hope. The measures for its
stamping out, though simple on paper, present difficulties interwoven with the very
fabric of society, but they are not insuper-
able, and are gradually disappearing. It is
for this reason we urge you to join with
enthusiasm in the crusade ; remembering,
however, that only the prolonged and united
efforts, carried through several generations,
can place the disease in the same category
with typhus fever, typhoid and small-pox.

In the comedies and tragedies of life our

immutable human nature reacts very much as in the dawn of science, and yet, with a widening of knowledge, the lights and shadows of the landscape have shifted, and the picture is brighter. Nothing can bring back the hour when sin and disease were correlated as confidently as night and day; and how shall we assess the enormous gain of a new criterion, a new estimate of the value of man's life! There are tones in human sentiment to-day which the ancients never heard, which our fathers indeed heard but faintly, and that without recognising their significance. The human heart by which we live has been touched as with the wand of a Prospero. What availed the sceptred race! what the glory that was Greece, or the grandeur that was Rome! of what avail even has been the message of the gospel, while the people at large were haunted by fear and anxiety, stricken by the pestilence of the darkness and the sickness of the noon-day? The new socialism of Science with its definite mission cares not a rap for the theories of Karl Marx, of Ferdinand Lassalle, or of Henry George; still less for the dreams of Plato or of Sir Thomas

69

More—or at least only so far as they help to realise the well-being of the citizen. Nor is there need to fear that in weighing the world in our balance we may drain the sap of its life, so long as we materialise in the service of man those eternal principles on which life rests—moral fervour, liberty and justice.

The outlook for the world as represented by Mary and John, and Jennie and Tom has never been so hopeful. There is no place for despondency or despair. As for the dour dyspeptics in mind and morals who sit idly croaking like ravens,—let them come into the arena, let them wrestle for their flesh and blood against the principalities and powers represented by bad air and worse houses, by drink and disease, by needless pain, and by the loss annually to the State of thousands of valuable lives—let them fight for the day when a man's life shall be more precious than gold. Now, alas! the cheapness of life is every day's tragedy!

If in the memorable phrase of the Greek philosopher Prodicus, "That which benefits human life is God," we may see in this new gospel a link betwixt us and the crowning

70

race of those who eye to eye shall look on
knowledge, and in whose hand Nature shall
be an open book, an approach to the glorious
day of which Shelley sings so gloriously :

> Happiness
> And Science dawn though late upon the earth ;
> Peace cheers the mind, health renovates the frame ;
> Disease and pleasure cease to mingle here,
> Reason and passion cease to combat there,
> Whilst mind unfettered o'er the earth extends
> Its all-subduing energies, and wields
> The sceptre of a vast dominion there.

A WAY OF LIFE

THE SALUTATION OF THE DAWN

Listen to the Exhortation of the Dawn !
　　Look to this Day !
For it is Life, the very Life of Life.
In its brief course lie all the
Varieties and Realities of your Existence :
　　　The Bliss of Growth,
　　　The Glory of Action,
　　　The Splendour of Beauty ;
For Yesterday is but a Dream,
And To-morrow is only a Vision,
　　But To-day well lived makes
Every Yesterday a Dream of Happiness,
And every To-morrow a Vision of Hope.
Look well, therefore, to this Day !
Such is the Salutation of the Dawn.

> Anon., " Words in Pain," 1919,
> frontispiece (from the Sanskrit).

What each day needs that shalt thou ask,
Each day will set its proper task.
> GOETHE.

EVERY man has a philosophy of life in thought, in word, or in deed, worked out in himself unconsciously. In possession of the very best, he may not know of its existence ; with the very worst he may pride himself as a paragon. As it grows with the growth it cannot be taught to the young in formal lectures. What have bright eyes, red blood, quick breath and taut muscles to do with philosophy ? Did not the great Stagirite say that young men were unfit students of it ?—they will hear as though they heard not, and to no profit. Why then should I trouble you ? Because I have a message that may be helpful. It is not philosophical, nor is it strictly moral or religious, one or other of which I was told my address should be, and yet in a way it is all three. It is the oldest and the freshest, the simplest and the most useful, so simple indeed is it that some of you may turn away disappointed as was Naaman the Syrian when told to go wash in Jordan and be

75

clean. You know those composite tools, to be bought for 50 cents, with one handle to fit a score or more of instruments. The workmanship is usually bad, so bad, as a rule, that you will not find an example in any good carpenter's shop ; but the boy has one, the chauffeur slips one into his box, and the sailor into his kit, and there is one in the odds-and-ends drawer of the pantry of every well-regulated family. It is simply a handy thing about the house, to help over the many little difficulties of the day. Of this sort of philosophy I wish to make you a present—a handle to fit your life tools. Whether the workmanship is Sheffield or shoddy, this helve will fit anything from a hatchet to a corkscrew.

My message is but a word, *a Way*, an easy expression of the experience of a plain man whose life has never been worried by any philosophy higher than that of the shepherd in *As You Like It*. I wish to point out a path in which the wayfaring man, though a fool, cannot err ; not a system to be worked out painfully only to be discarded, not a formal scheme, simply a habit as easy—or as hard ! —to adopt as any other habit, good or bad.

76

I

A few years ago a Xmas card went the rounds, with the legend " Life is just one ' derned ' thing after another," which, in more refined language, is the same as saying " Life is a habit," a succession of actions that become more or less automatic. This great truth, which lies at the basis of all actions, muscular or psychic, is the keystone of the teaching of Aristotle, to whom the formation of habits was the basis of moral excellence. " In a word, habits of any kind are the result of actions of the same kind ; and so what we have to do, is to give a certain character to these particular actions " (*Ethics*). Lift a seven months old baby to his feet—see him tumble on his nose. Do the same at twelve months—he walks. At two years he runs. The muscles and the nervous system have acquired the habit. One trial after another, one failure after another, has given him power. Put your finger in a baby's mouth, and he sucks away in blissful anticipation of a response to a mammalian habit millions of years old. And we can deliberately train parts of our body to perform complicated actions with unerring accuracy. Watch that musician playing a difficult piece. Batteries, commutators, multipliers, switches, wires innumerable control those nimble fingers, the machinery of which may be set in motion as automatically as in a pianola, the player all the time chatting as if he had nothing to do in controlling the apparatus—habit again, the gradual acquisition of power by long practice and at the expense of many mistakes. The same great law reaches through mental and moral states. " Character," which partakes of both, in Plutarch's words, is " long-standing habit."

Now the way of life that I preach is a habit to be acquired gradually by long and steady repetition. It is the practice of living for the day only, and for the day's work, *Life in day-tight compartments.* " Ah," I hear you say, " that is an easy matter, simple as Elisha's advice ! " Not as I shall urge it, in words which fail to express the depth of my feelings as to its value. I started life in the best of all environments—in a parsonage, one of nine children. A man who has filled Chairs in four universities, has written a successful book, and has been asked to lecture at Yale, is supposed popularly to have brains of a special quality. A few of my intimate friends really know the truth about me, as I know it! Mine, in good faith I say it, are of the most mediocre character. But what about those professorships, etc.? Just habit, a way of life, an outcome of the day's work, the vital importance of which I wish to impress upon you with all the force at my command.

Dr. Johnson remarked upon the trifling circumstances by which men's lives are influenced, " not by an ascendant planet, a predominating humour, but by the first book which they read, some early conversation which they have heard, or some accident which excited ardour and enthusiasm." This was my case in two particulars. I was diverted to the Trinity College School, then at Weston, Ontario, by a paragraph in the circular stating that the senior boys would go into the drawing-room in the evenings, and learn to sing and dance—vocal and pedal accomplishments for which I was never designed ; but like Saul seeking his asses, I found something more valuable, a man of the White of Selborne type, who knew nature, and who knew how to get boys interested in it.* The other happened in the summer of 1871, when I was attending the Montreal General Hospital. Much worried as to the future, partly about the final examination, partly as to what I should do afterwards, I picked up a volume of Carlyle, and on the page I opened there was the familiar sentence—" *Our main business is not to see what lies dimly at a distance, but to do what lies clearly at hand.*" A commonplace sentiment enough, but it hit and stuck and helped, and was the starting-point of a habit that has enabled me to utilise to the full the single talent entrusted to me.

II

The workers in Christ's vineyard were hired by the day ; only for this day are we to ask for our daily bread, and we are expressly bidden to take no thought for the morrow. To the modern world these commands have

* The Rev. W. A. Johnson, the founder of the school.

an Oriental savour, counsels of perfection
akin to certain of the Beatitudes, stimuli to
aspiration, not to action. I am prepared on
the contrary to urge the literal acceptance of
the advice, not in the mood of St. James—
" Go to now, ye that say, To-day or to-
morrow we will go into such a city, and
continue there a year, and buy and sell, and
get gain : whereas ye know not what shall
be on the morrow " ; not in the Epicurean
spirit of Omar with his " jug of wine and
thou," but in the modernist spirit, as a way
of life, a habit, a strong enchantment at once
against the mysticism of the East and the
pessimism that too easily besets us. Change
that hard saying " Sufficient unto the day is
the evil thereof " into " the goodness
thereof," since the chief worries of life arise
from the foolish habit of looking before and
after. As a patient with double vision from
some transient unequal action of the muscles
of the eye finds magical relief from well-
adjusted glasses, so, returning to the clear
binocular vision of to-day, the over-anxious
student finds peace when he looks neither
backward to the past nor forward to the
future.

G

I stood on the bridge of one of the great
liners, ploughing the ocean at 25 knots.
" She is alive," said my companion, " in
every plate ; a huge monster with brain and
nerves, an immense stomach, a wonderful
heart and lungs, and a splendid system of
locomotion." Just at that moment a signal
sounded, and all over the ship the water-
tight compartments were closed. " Our
chief factor of safety," said the Captain.
" In spite of the *Titanic*," I said. " Yes,"
he replied, " in spite of the *Titanic*." Now
each one of you is a much more marvellous
organisation than the great liner, and bound
on a longer voyage. What I urge is that
you so learn to control the machinery as to
live with " day-tight compartments " as the
most certain way to ensure safety on the
voyage. Get on the bridge, and see that
at least the great bulkheads are in working
order. Touch a button and hear, at every
level of your life, the iron doors shutting out
the Past—the dead yesterdays. Touch another and shut off, with a metal curtain, the
Future—the unborn to-morrows. Then you
are safe,—safe for to-day ! Read the old
story in the *Chambered Nautilus*, so beauti-
82

fully sung by Oliver Wendell Holmes, only
change one line to " Day after day beheld
the silent toil." Shut off the past! Let the
dead past bury its dead. So easy to say, so
hard to realise! The truth is, the past
haunts us like a shadow. To disregard it is
not easy. Those blue eyes of your grand-
mother, that weak chin of your grandfather,
have mental and moral counterparts in your
make-up. Generations of ancestors, brood-
ing over " Providence, foreknowledge, will
and fate, Fixed fate, free will, foreknowledge
absolute," may have bred a New England
conscience, morbidly sensitive, to heal which
some of you had rather sing the 51st Psalm
than follow Christ into the slums. Shut out
the yesterdays, which have lighted fools the
way to dusty death, and have no concern for
you personally, that is, consciously. They
are there all right, working daily in us, but so
are our livers and our stomachs. And the
past, in its unconscious action on our lives,
should bother us as little as they do. The
petty annoyances, the real and fancied
slights, the trivial mistakes, the disappoint-
ments, the sins, the sorrows, even the joys—
bury them deep in the oblivion of each

night. Ah! but it is just then that to so
many of us the ghosts of the past,

Night-riding Incubi
Troubling the fantasy,

come in troops, and pry open the eyelids,
each one presenting a sin, a sorrow, a regret.
Bad enough in the old and seasoned, in the
young these demons of past sins may be a
terrible affliction, and in bitterness of heart
many a one cries with Eugene Aram, " Oh
God! Could I so close my mind, and clasp
it with a clasp." As a vaccine against all
morbid poisons left in the system by the
infections of yesterday, I offer " a way of
life." " Undress," as George Herbert says,
" your soul at night," not by self-examina-
tion, but by shedding, as you do your
garments, the daily sins whether of omission
or of commission, and you will wake a free
man, with a new life. To look back, except
on rare occasions for stock-taking, is to risk
the fate of Lot's wife. Many a man is
handicapped in his course by a cursed
combination of retro- and intro-spection, the
mistakes of yesterday paralysing the efforts
of to-day, the worries of the past hugged to

his destruction, and the worm Regret allowed to canker the very heart of his life. To die daily, after the manner of St. Paul, ensures the resurrection of a new man, who makes each day the epitome of a life.

III

The load of to-morrow, added to that of yesterday, carried to-day makes the strongest falter. Shut off the future as tightly as the past. No dreams, no visions, no delicious fantasies, no castles in the air, with which, as the old song so truly says, " hearts are broken, heads are turned." To youth, we are told, belongs the future, but the wretched to-morrow that so plagues some of us has no certainty, except through to-day. Who can tell what a day may bring forth ? Though its uncertainty is a proverb, a man may carry its secret in the hollow of his hand. Make a pilgrimage to Hades with Ulysses, draw the magic circle, perform the rites, and then ask Tiresias the question. I have had the answer from his own lips. The future is to-day,—there is no to-morrow ! The day of a man's salvation is *now*—the life of the present, of to-day, lived earnestly, intently, without a forward-looking thought, is the only insurance for the future. Let the limit of your horizon be a twenty-four hour circle. On the title page of one of the great books of science, the *Discours de la Méthode* of Descartes (1637), is a vignette showing a man digging in a garden with his face towards the earth, on which rays of light are streaming from the heavens; above him is the legend " *Fac et Spera.*" 'Tis a good attitude and a good motto. Look heavenward, if you wish, but never to the horizon—that way danger lies. Truth is not there, happiness is not there, certainty is not there, but the falsehoods, the frauds, the quackeries, the *ignes fatui* which have deceived each generation—all beckon from the horizon, and lure the men not content to look for the truth and happiness that tumble out at their feet. Once while at College climb a mountain-top, and get a general outlook of the land, and make it the occasion perhaps of that careful examination of yourself, that inquisition which Descartes urges every man to hold once in a lifetime—not oftener.

Waste of energy, mental distress, nervous

worries dog the steps of a man who is anxious about the future. Shut close, then, the great fore and aft bulkheads, and prepare to cultivate the habit of a life of Day-Tight Compartments. Do not be discouraged,— like every other habit, the acquisition takes time, and the way is one you must find for yourselves. I can only give general directions and encouragement, in the hope that while the green years are on your heads, you may have the courage to persist.

IV

Now, for the day itself! What first? Be your own daysman! and sigh not with Job for any mysterious intermediary, but prepare to lay your own firm hand upon the helm. Get into touch with the finite, and grasp in full enjoyment that sense of capacity in a machine working smoothly. Join the whole creation of animate things in a deep, heartfelt joy that you are alive, that you see the sun, that you are in this glorious earth which nature has made so beautiful, and which is yours to conquer and to enjoy. Realise, in the words of Browning, that

87

" There's a world of capability for joy spread round about us, meant for us, inviting us." What are the morning sensations ?— for they control the day. Some of us are congenitally unhappy during the early hours; but the young man who feels on awakening that life is a burden or a bore has been neglecting his machine, driving it too hard, stoking the engines too much, or not cleaning out the ashes and clinkers. Or he has been too much with the Lady Nicotine, or fooling with Bacchus, or, worst of all, with the younger Aphrodite—all " messengers of strong prevailment in unhardened youth." To have a sweet outlook on life you must have a clean body. As I look on the clear-cut, alert, earnest features, and the lithe, active forms of our college men, I sometimes wonder whether or not Socrates and Plato would find the race improved. I am sure they would love to look on such a gathering as this. Make their ideal yours—the fair mind in the fair body. The one cannot be sweet and clean without the other, and you must realise, with Rabbi Ben Ezra, the great truth that flesh and soul are mutually helpful. The morning outlook—which really makes

the day—is largely a question of a clean
machine—of physical morality in the wide
sense of the term. " *C'est l'estomac qui fait
les heureux,*" as Voltaire says ; no dyspeptic
can have a sane outlook on life ; and a man
whose bodily functions are impaired has a
lowered moral resistance. To keep the body
fit is a help in keeping the mind pure, and
the sensations of the first few hours of the
day are the best test of its normal state. The
clean tongue, the clear head, and the bright
eye are birth-rights of each day.   Just as the
late Professor Marsh would diagnose an
unknown animal from a single bone, so can
the day be predicted from the first waking
hour.   The start is everything, as you well
know, and to make a good start you must
feel fit.   In the young, sensations of morning
slackness come most often from lack of
control of the two primal instincts—biologic
habits—the one concerned with the preser-
vation of the individual, the other with the
continuance of the species. Yale students
should by this time be models of dietetic
propriety, but youth does not always reck
the rede of the teacher ; and I dare say that
here, as elsewhere, careless habits of eating

are responsible for much mental disability.
My own rule of life has been to cut out
unsparingly any article of diet that had the
bad taſte to disagree with me, or to indicate
in any way that it had abused the temporary
hospitality of the lodging which I had
provided. To drink, nowadays, but few
ſtudents become addicted, but in every large
body of men a few are to be found whose
incapacity for the day results from the
morning clogging of nocturnally-flushed
tissues. As moderation is very hard to
reach, and as it has been abundantly shown
that the beſt of mental and physical work
may be done without alcohol in any form,
the safeſt rule for the young man is that
which I am sure moſt of you follow—
abſtinence. A bitter enemy to the bright
eye and the clear brain of the early morning
is tobacco when smoked to excess, as it is
now by a large majority of ſtudents. Watch
it, teſt it, and if need be, control it. That
befogged, woolly sensation reaching from
the forehead to the occiput, that haziness of
memory, that cold fish-like eye, that furred
tongue, and laſt week's taſte in the mouth—
too many of you know them—I know them

90

—they often come from too much tobacco. The other primal instinct is the heavy burden of the flesh which Nature puts on all of us to ensure a continuation of the species. To drive Plato's team taxes the energies of the best of us. One of the horses is a raging, untamed devil, who can only be brought into subjection by hard fighting and severe training. This much you all know as men : once the bit is between his teeth the black steed Passion will take the white horse Reason with you and the chariot rattling over the rocks to perdition.

With a fresh, sweet body you can start aright without those feelings of inertia that so often, as Goethe says, make the morning's lazy leisure usher in a useless day. Control of the mind as a working machine, the adaptation in it of habit, so that its action becomes almost as automatic as walking, is the end of education—and yet how rarely reached ! It can be accomplished with deliberation and repose, never with hurry and worry. Realise how much time there is, how long the day is. Realise that you have sixteen waking hours, three or four of which at least should be devoted to making a silent

conquest of your mental machinery. Concentration, by which is grown gradually the
power to wrestle successfully with any
subject, is the secret of successful study. No
mind however dull can escape the brightness
that comes from steady application. There
is an old saying, " Youth enjoyeth not, for
haste " ; but worse than this, the failure to
cultivate the power of peaceful concentration
is the greatest single cause of mental breakdown. Plato pities the young man who
started at such a pace that he never reached
the goal. One of the saddest of life's
tragedies is the wreckage of the career of the
young collegian by hurry, hustle, bustle and
tension—the human machine driven day and
night, as no sensible fellow would use his
motor. Listen to the words of a master in
Israel, William James : " Neither the nature
nor the amount of our work is accountable
for the frequency and severity of our break-
downs, but their cause lies rather in those
absurd feelings of hurry and having no time,
in that breathlessness and tension, that
anxiety of feature and that solicitude of
results, that lack of inner harmony and ease,
in short, by which the work with us is apt

to be accompanied, and from which a European who would do the same work would, nine out of ten times, be free." *Es bildet ein Talent sich in der Stille,* but it need not be for all day. A few hours out of the sixteen will suffice, only let them be hours of daily dedication—in routine, in order and in system, and day by day you will gain in power over the mental mechanism, just as the child does over the spinal marrow in walking, or the musician over the nerve centres. Aristotle somewhere says that the student who wins out in the fight must be slow in his movements, with voice deep, and slow speech, and he will not be worried over trifles which make people speak in shrill tones and use rapid movements. Shut close in hour-tight compartments, with the mind directed intensely upon the subject in hand, you will acquire the capacity to do more and more, you will get into training ; and once the mental habit is established, you are safe for life.

Concentration is an art of slow acquisition, but little by little the mind is accustomed to habits of slow eating and careful digestion, by which alone you escape the " mental dyspepsy " so graphically described by Lowell in the *Fable for Critics*. Do not worry your brains about that bugbear Efficiency, which, sought consciously and with effort, is just one of those elusive qualities very apt to be missed. The man's college output is never to be gauged at sight ; all the world's coarse thumb and finger may fail to plumb his most effective work, the casting of the mental machinery of self-education, the true preparation for a field larger than the college campus. Four or five hours daily—it is not much to ask ; but one day must tell another, one week certify another, one month bear witness to another of the same story, and you will acquire a habit by which the one-talent man will earn a high interest, and by which the ten-talent man may at least save his capital.

Steady work of this sort gives a man a sane outlook on the world. No corrective so valuable to the weariness, the fever and the fret that are so apt to wring the heart of the young. This is the talisman, as George Herbert says,

> The famous stone
> That turneth all to gold,

94

and with which, to the eternally recurring question, What is Life? you answer, I do not think—I act it; the only philosophy that brings you in contact with its real values and enables you to grasp its hidden meaning. Over the Slough of Despond, past Doubting Castle and Giant Despair, with this talisman you may reach the Delectable Mountains, and those Shepherds of the Mind—Knowledge, Experience, Watchful and Sincere. Some of you may think this to be a miserable Epicurean doctrine—no better than that so sweetly sung by Horace :—

Happy the man—and Happy he alone,
He who can call to-day his own,
He who secure within can say,
To-morrow, do thy worst—for I have lived to-day.

I do not care what you think, I am simply giving you a philosophy of life that I have found helpful in my work, useful in my play. Walt Whitman, whose physician I was for some years, never spoke to me much of his poems, though occasionally he would make a quotation ; but I remember late one summer afternoon as we sat in the window of his little house in Camden there passed a group of workmen whom he greeted in his usual friendly way. And then he said : " Ah, the glory of the day's work, whether with hand or brain ! I have tried

> To exalt the present and the real,
> To teach the average man the glory of his daily work
>   or trade."

In this way of life each one of you may learn to drive the straight furrow and so come to the true measure of a man.

V

With body and mind in training, what remains ?

Do you remember that most touching of all incidents in Christ's ministry, when the anxious ruler Nicodemus came by night, worried lest the things that pertained to his everlasting peace were not a part of his busy and successful life ? Christ's message to him is His message to the world—never more needed than at present : " Ye must be born of the spirit." You wish to be with the leaders—as Yale men it is your birthright— know the great souls that make up the moral radium of the world. You must be born of

96

their spirit, initiated into their fraternity, whether of the spiritually-minded followers of the Nazarene or of that larger company, elect from every nation, seen by St. John.

Begin the day with Christ and His prayer —you need no other. Creedless, with it you have religion ; creed-stuffed, it will leaven any theological dough in which you stick. As the soul is dyed by the thoughts, let no day pass without contact with the best literature of the world. Learn to know your Bible, though not perhaps as your fathers did. In forming character and in shaping conduct, its touch has still its ancient power. Of the kindred of Ram and sons of Elihu, you should know its beauties and its strength. Fifteen or twenty minutes day by day will give you fellowship with the great minds of the race, and little by little as the years pass you extend your friendship with the immortal dead. They will give you faith in your own day. Listen while they speak to you of the fathers. But each age has its own spirit and ideas, just as it has its own manners and pleasures. You are right to believe that yours is the best University, at its best period. Why should you look back to be shocked at the frowsiness and dullness of the students of the seventies or even of the nineties ? And cast no thought forward, lest you reach a period when you and yours will present to your successors the same dowdiness of clothes and times. But while change is the law, certain great ideas flow fresh through the ages, and control us effectually as in the days of Pericles. Mankind, it has been said, is always advancing, man is always the same. The love, hope, fear and faith that make humanity, and the elemental passions of the human heart, remain unchanged, and the secret of inspiration in any literature is the capacity to touch the cord that vibrates in a sympathy that knows nor time nor place.

The quiet life in day-tight compartments will help you to bear your own and others' burdens with a light heart. Pay no heed to the Batrachians who sit croaking idly by the stream. Life is a straight, plain business, and the way is clear, blazed for you by generations of strong men, into whose labours you enter and whose ideals must be your inspiration. In my mind's eye I can see you twenty years hence—resolute-eyed, broad-headed, smooth-faced men who are in the world to make a success of life ; but to whichever of the two great types you belong, whether controlled by emotion or by reason, you will need the leaven of their spirit, the only leaven potent enough to avert that only too common Nemesis to which the Psalmist refers : " He gave them their heart's desire, but sent leanness withal into their souls."

I quoted Dr. Johnson's remark about the trivial things that influence. Perhaps this slight word of mine may help some of you so to number your days that you may apply your hearts unto wisdom.

SCIENCE AND IMMORTALITY

In all ages no problem has so stretched to aching the *pia mater* of the thoughtful man as that put in such simple words by Job, "If a man die, shall he live again?" Appreciating the fact that a question of such eternal significance presents special aspects at special periods, Miss Caroline Haskell Ingersoll founded this lectureship in memory of her father, George Goldthwait Ingersoll, of the class of 1805. Knowing that the days were evil and the generation perverse, and imitating, perhaps, the satiric touch in Dean Swift's famous legacy,[1] she made this community the recipient of her bounty.

To attempt to say anything on immortality seems presumptuous—a subject on which everything possible has been said before, and so well said, not only by the master-minds of the race, but by the many, far wiser than I, who have spoken from this place. But having declined the honour once, and having learned from President Eliot that others of my profession had also

declined, when a second invitation came it
seemed ungracious, even cowardly, not to
accept, though at the present moment, before
so distinguished an audience, I cannot but
envy the discretion of my friends, and with
such a task ahead I feel as Childe Roland
must have felt before the Dark Tower.

One of my colleagues, hearing that I was
to give this lecture, said to me, " What do
you know about immortality ? You will
say a few pleasant things, and quote the
Religio Medici, but there will be nothing
certain." In truth, with his wonted felicity,
my life-long mentor, Sir Thomas Browne,
has put the problem very well when he said
in *Urn Burial*, " A dialogue between two
infants in the womb concerning the state of
this world might handsomely illustrate our
ignorance of the next, whereof, methinks, we
yet discourse in Plato's den—the cave of
transitive shadows—and are but embryon
philosophers." Than the physician, no one
has a better opportunity to study the attitude
of mind of his fellow-men on the problem.
Others, perhaps, get nearer to John, taking
no thought for the morrow, as he disports
himself in the pride of life ; but who gets so

near to the real John as known to his Maker, to John in sickness and in sorrow and sore perplexed as to the future ? * The physician's work lies on the confines of the shadow-land, and it might be expected that, if to any, to him would come glimpses that might make us less forlorn when in the bitterness of loss we cry, as in Tennyson's *Maud*—

> Ah, Christ ! that it were possible
> For one short hour to see
> The souls we loved, that they might tell us
> What and where they be !

Neither a philosopher nor the son of a philosopher, I miss the lofty vantage-ground of a prolonged training in things of the spirit enjoyed by my predecessors in this lectureship, but to approach the problem from the standpoint of a man, part at least of whose training has been in the habit and faculty of observation, as Aristotle defines science, and whose philosophy of life is as frankly pragmatic as that of the shepherd in *As You Like It*,² may help to keep a discussion of the incomprehensible within the limits of the intelligence of a popular audience.

* *Autocrat of the Breakfast Table.*

Within the lifetime of some of us, Science
—physical, chemical, and biological—has
changed the aspect of the world, changed it
more effectively and more permanently than
all the efforts of man in all preceding
generations. Living in it, we cannot fully
appreciate the transformation, and we are
too close to the events to realise their
tremendous significance. The control of
physical energies, the biological revolution,
and the good start which has been made in a
warfare against disease, were the three great
achievements of the nineteenth century, each
one of which has had a profound and far-
reaching influence on almost every relation-
ship in the life of man. And, not knowing
what a day may bring forth, we have
entered upon another century in an attitude
of tremulous expectation, and with a feeling
of confidence that the coöperation of many
labourers in many fields will yield a still
richer harvest. It may be asked at the outset
whether the subject be one with which
science has anything to do, except on the
broad principle of the famous maxim of
Terence, " *Homo sum ; humani nihil a me
alienum puto.*" Goethe remarked that " man-

kind is always advancing ; man always remains the same ; science deals with mankind," and it may be of interest to inquire whether, in regard to a belief in a future life, mankind's conquest of nature has made the individual more or less hopeful of a life beyond the grave.

A scientific observer, freeing his mind, as far as possible, from the bonds of education and environment, so as to make an impartial study of the problem, would be helped at the outset by the old triple classification, which fits our modern conditions just as it has those of all ages ; and I shall make it serve as a framework for this lecture. While accepting a belief in immortality, and accepting the phases and forms of the prevailing religion, an immense majority live practically uninfluenced by it, except in so far as it ministers to a wholesale dissonance between the inner and the outer life, and diffuses an atmosphere of general insincerity. A second group, larger, perhaps, to-day than ever before in history, put the supernatural altogether out of man's life, and regard the hereafter as only one of the many inventions he has sought out for himself. A third group, ever small and select, lay hold with the anchor of faith upon eternal life as the controlling influence in this one.

I

THE LAODICEANS

The desire for immortality seems never to have had a very strong hold upon mankind, and the belief is less widely held than is usually stated, but on this part of the question time will not permit me to do more than to make, in passing, a remark or two. Even to our masters, the Greeks, the future life was a shadowy existence. " Whether they really partake of any good or evil? " asks Aristotle of the dead. Who does not sympathise with the lament of Achilles, stalking among the shades and envying the lowliest swain on earth? * " It harrows us with fear and wonder," as Jowett says, speaking of Buddhism, " to learn that this vast system, numerically the most universal or catholic of all religions, and in many of its leading features most like Christianity, is

* *Odyssey, Book XI.*

based, not on the hope of eternal life, but of complete annihilation." [3] " And the educated Chinaman looks for no personal immortality, but the generations past and the generations to come form with those that are alive one single whole ; all live eternally, though it is only some that happen at any moment to live upon earth." [4]

Practical indifference is the modern attitude of mind ; we are Laodiceans,—neither hot nor cold, but lukewarm, as a very superficial observation will make plain. The natural man has only two primal passions, to get and beget,—to get the means of sustenance (and to-day a little more) and to beget his kind. Satisfy these, and he looks neither before nor after, but goeth forth to his work and to his labour until the evening, and returning, sweats in oblivion without a thought of whence or whither. At one end of the scale the gay and giddy Cyrenaic rout—the society set of the modern world, which repeats with wearisome monotony the same old vices and the same old follies—cares not a fig for the life to come. Let us eat and drink ; let us enjoy every hour saved from that eternal silence. " There be delights," to quote Milton's *Areopagitica*, "there be recreations and jolly pastimes that will fetch the day about from sun to sun, and rock the tedious year as in a delightful dream." [5] Even our more sober friends, as we see them day by day, interested in stocks and strikes, in base-ball and "bridge," arrange their view of this world entirely regardless of what may be beyond the flaming barriers—*flammantia mœnia mundi*. Where, among the educated and refined, much less among the masses, do we find any ardent desire for a future life? It is not a subject of drawing-room conversation, and the man whose habit it is to buttonhole his acquaintances and inquire earnestly after their souls, is shunned like the Ancient Mariner. Among the clergy it is not thought polite to refer to so delicate a topic except officially from the pulpit. Most ominous of all, as indicating the utter absence of interest on the part of the public, is the silence of the Press, in the columns of which are manifest daily the works of the flesh. Any active demand for a presentation of the spiritual and of the "unseen" would require that they should sow to the spirit and bring forth the fruits of the spirit. On special occasions only, in sickness and in sorrow, or in the presence of some great catastrophe, do disturbing thoughts arise: " Whence are we, and why are we ? Of what scene the actors or spectators ? " * and man's heart grows cold at the thought that he must die, and that upon him, too, the worms shall feed sweetly. Few among the religious can reproach themselves, as did Donne, with an over-earnest desire for the next life, and those few have the same cause as had the Divine Dean—a burden of earthly cares too grievous to be borne. The lip-sigh of discontent, when in full health, at a too prolonged stay in Kedar's tents changes quickly, in sickness, to the strong cry of Hezekiah as he drew near to the gates of the grave. And the eventide of life is not always hopeful ; on the contrary, the older we grow, the less fixed, very often, is the belief in a future life. Waller's bimundane prospect [6] is rarely seen to-day. As Howells tells us of Lowell,[7] " His hold upon a belief in life after death weakened with his years." Like Oliver Wendell Holmes, " we may love

* Shelley, *Adonais*.

the mystical and talk much of the shadows, but when it comes to going out among them and laying hold of them with the hand of faith, we are not of the excursion." [8]

If among individuals we find little but indifference to this great question, what shall we say to the national and public sentiment? Immortality, and all that it may mean, is a dead issue in the great movements of the world. In the social and political forces what account is taken by practical men of any eternal significance in life? Does it ever enter into the consideration of those controlling the destinies of their fellow-creatures that this life is only a preparation for another? To raise the question is to raise a smile. I am not talking of our professions, but of the every-day condition which only serves to emphasise the contrast between the precepts of the gospel and the practice of the street. Without a peradventure it may be said that a living faith in a future existence has not the slightest influence in the settlement of the grave social and national problems which confront the race to-day.

Then, again, we habitually talk of the departed, not as though they had passed

from death unto life, and were in a state of
conscious joy and felicity, or otherwise, but
we count them out of our circle with set
deliberation, and fix between them and us a
gulf as deep as that which separated Dives
from Lazarus. That sweet and gracious
feeling of an ever-present immortality, so
keenly appreciated in the religion of Numa,
has no meaning for us. The dead are no
longer immanent, and we have lost that
sense of continuity which the Romans
expressed so touchingly in their private
festivals of the Ambarvalia, in which the
dead were invoked and remembered.* Even
that golden chord of Catholic doctrine, the
Communion of the Saints, so comforting
to the faithful in all ages, is worn to a
thread in our working-day world. Over
our fathers immortality brooded like the
day ; we have consciously thrust it out of
lives so full and busy that we have no
time to make an enduring covenant with
our dead.

Another reason, perhaps, for popular indifference is the vague mistiness of the picture
of the future life, the uncertainty neces-

* Walter Pater, *Marius the Epicurean.*

sarily pertaining to the things that "eye
hath not seen nor ear heard, neither have
entered into the heart of man to conceive,"
the absence of features in the presentation
which prove attractive, and the presence of
others most repulsive to the Western spirit.
What is there in the description of the
Apocalypse to appeal to the matter-of-fact
occidental mind ? The infinite monotony of
the oriental presentation repels rather than
attracts, and the sober aspirations of Socrates
are more appreciated than the ecstasies of
St. John. Commenting upon this, Jowett, in
the introduction to *Phædo*, says, " And yet to
beings constituted as we are, the monotony
of singing psalms would be as great an
affliction as the pains of hell, and might be
even pleasantly interrupted by them." How
little account is taken of our changed attitude
of mind on these questions !

Emerson somewhere remarks that the
cheapness of man is every day's tragedy, and
the way human life has been cheapened in
our Western civilisation illustrates practically
how far we are from any thought of a future
existence. Had we any deep conviction that
the four thousand persons who were killed

laśt year on the railways of this country,[9] and the nine thousand who met with violent deaths, were living souls whose śtatus in eternity depended on their belief at the moment when they were sent to their account "unrespited, unpitied, unreprieved," —had we, I say, any earneśt conviċtion of this, would not the hearts of this people be knit together in a fcrvid uprising such as that which brought deśtruċtion upon Benjamin, in the matter of a certain Levite sojourning on the side of Mount Ephraim ? (Judges xix, xx). Think, too, of the countless thousands of the Innocents made to pass through the fire to the Moloch of civic inefficiency ! Of the thousands of young men and maidens sacrificed annually to that modern Minotaur—typhoid fever ! We intelleċtuals, too, bear the brand of Cain upon our foreheads, and cull out our college holidays with gladiatorial conteśts which laśt year cośt the lives of thirty-five young fellows, and brutally maimed other five hundred.[10]   Rend the veil of familiarity through which we look at this bloody record, this wholesale slaughter, and cold chill will śtrike the marrow of any thought-

ful man, and he will murmur in shame with
Horace:—

> Eheu! cicatricum et sceleris pudet
> Fratrumque. Quid nos dura refugimus
> Aetas? quid intactum nefasti
>   Liquimus? unde manum juventus
> Metu deorum continuit.[11]

To the scientific student there is much of
interest in what Milton calls this business of
death,* which of all human things alone is a
plain case and admits of no controversy,
and one aspect of it relates directly to the
problem before us. The popular belief that
however careless a man may be while in
health, at least on the " low, dark verge of
life," he is appalled at the prospect of leaving
these warm precincts to go he knows not
where—this popular belief is erroneous.
As a rule, man dies as he has lived, uninfluenced practically by the thought of a
future life. Bunyan could not understand
the quiet, easy death of Mr. Badman, and
took it as an incontestible sign of his
damnation. The ideal death of Cornelius, so
beautifully described in the Colloquies of
Erasmus, is rarely seen. In our modern life

* *Eikonoklastes.*

the educated man dies usually as did Mr.
Denner in Margaret Deland's *John Ward,
Preacher*—wondering, but uncertain, gene-
rally unconscious and unconcerned.[12]   I
have careful records of about five hundred
death-beds, studied particularly with refer-
ence to the modes of death and the sensations
of the dying.   The latter alone concern
us here.   Ninety suffered bodily pain or
distress of one sort or another, eleven
showed mental apprehension, two positive
terror, one expressed spiritual exaltation,
one bitter remorse.   The great majority gave
no signs one way or the other ; like their
birth, their death was a sleep and a forgetting.
The Preacher was right ; in this matter man
hath no preëminence over the beast—" as
the one dieth so dieth the other."

Take wings of fancy, and ascend with
Icaromenippus, and sit between him and
Empedocles on a ledge in the moon,
whence you can get a panoramic view
of the ant - like life of man on this
world.   What will you see ?   Busy with
domestic and personal duties, absorbed in
civic and commercial pursuits, striving and
straining for better or worse in state and

national affairs, wrangling and fighting between the dwellers in the neighbouring
ant-hills—everywhere a scene of restless
activity as the hungry generations tread each
other down in their haste to the goal, but
nowhere will you see any evidence of an
overwhelming, dominant, absorbing passion
regulating the life of man because he believes
this world to be only the training-ground
for another and a better one. And this is the
most enduring impression a scientific observer would obtain from an impartial view
of the situation to-day.

II

THE GALLIONIANS

The great bulk of the people are lukewarm Laodiceans, concerned less with the
future life than with the price of beef or coal.
Our scientific student, scanning his fellow-
men, would soon recognise the second
group, the Gallionians, who deliberately
put the matter aside as one about which we
know nothing and have no means of knowing anything. Like Gallio, in the Acts, they

118

care for none of these things, and live wholly
uninfluenced by a thought of the hereafter.
They have either reached the intellectual
conviction that there is no hope in the grave,
or the question remains open, as it did with
Darwin, and the absorbing interests of other
problems and the every-day calls of domestic
life satisfy the mind. It was my privilege to
know well one of the greatest naturalists of
this country, Joseph Leidy, who reached
this standpoint, and I have often heard him
say that the question of a future state had long
ceased to interest him or to have any influence
in his life. I think there can be no doubt
that this attitude of mind is more common
among naturalists and investigators than in
men devoted to literature and the humanities.

Science may be said to have at least four
points of contact with a belief in immortality. In the first place, it has caused a
profound change in men's thoughts within
the past generation. The introduction of a
new factor has modified the views of man's
origin, of his place in nature, and, in conse-
quence, of his destiny. The belief of our
fathers may be expressed in the fewest
possible words : " For as in Adam all die,

even so in Christ shall all be made alive."
Man was an *angelus sepultus* (Donne, *Biatha-natos*) which had—

Forsook the courts of everlasting day,
And chose with us a darksome house of mortal
clay.*

Created in the image of God, " sufficient to
have stood though free to fall," (*Paradise
Lost*), he fell, and is an outlaw from his
father's house, to which he is now privileged
to return at the price of the Son of God.
This is the Sunday story from orthodox
pulpits, and it is what we teach to our
children. On the other hand, to science
man is the one far-off event towards which
the whole creation has moved, the crowning
glory of organic life, the end-product of a
ceaseless evolution which has gone on for
æons, since in some early Pelagian sea life
first appeared, whence and how science
knows not. The week-day story tells of
man, not a degenerate descendant of the
sons of the gods, but the heir of all the ages,
with head erect and brow serene, confident
in himself, confident in the future, as he

* Milton, *Hymn on the Nativity*.

pursues the gradual paths of an aspiring change. How profoundly the problem of man's destiny and of his relation to the unseen world has been affected by science is seen in the current literature of the day, which expresses the naturally irreconcilable breach between two such diametrically opposed views of his origin. But this has not been wholly a result of the biological revolution through which we have passed. The critical study of the Bible has weakened the belief in revelation, and so indirectly in immortality, and science has had a good deal to say about the credibility of what purports to be a direct revelation based on miracles. The younger ones among you cannot appreciate the mental cataclysm of the past forty years. The battle of Armageddon has been fought and lost, and many of the survivors, as they tread the *via dolorosa*, feel in aching scars

the bitter change
Of fierce extremes, extremes by change more fierce,—
(*Paradise Lost*)

the heavy change from the days when faith was diversified with doubt, to the present days, when doubt is diversified with faith.

121

Secondly, modern psychological science dispenses altogether with the soul. The old difficulty for which Socrates chided Cebes,* who feared, in the words of Matthew Arnold, that—

> the soul
> Which now is mine must reattain
> Immunity from my control,
> And wander round the world again,

this old dread, so hard to charm away, lest in tne vast and wandering air the homeless Animula might lose its identity, that eternal form would no longer divide eternal soul from all beside,—this difficulty science ignores altogether. The association of life in all its phases with organisation, the association of a gradation of intelligence with increasing complexity of organisation, the failure of the development of intelligence with an arrest in cerebral growth in the child, the slow decay of mind with changes in the brain, the absolute dependence of the higher mental attributes upon definite structures, the instantaneous loss of consciousness when the blood supply is cut off from the higher centres—these facts give pause to the

* Plato, *Phaedo*.

scientific student when he tries to think of intelligence apart from organisation.[13] Far, very far, from any rational explanation of thought as a condition of matter, why should he consider the, to him, unthinkable proposition of consciousness without a corresponding material basis ? The old position, so beautifully expressed in the *Religio Medici* by Sir Thomas Browne, " Thus we are men and we know not how : there is something in us that can be without us and will be after us ; though it is strange that it has no history what it was before us, nor cannot tell how it entered us,"—this old Platonic and orthodox view has no place in science, which ignores completely this something that will be after us. The new psychologists have ceased to think nobly of the soul, and even speak of it as a complete superfluity. There is much to suggest, and it is a pleasing fancy that outside our consciousness lie fields of psychical activity analogous to the invisible yet powerful rays of the spectrum. The thousand activities of the bodily machine, some of them noisy enough at times, do not in health obtrude themselves upon our consciousness, and just as there is this enormous subconscious field of vegetative life, so there may be a vast supra-conscious sphere of astral life,* the manifestations of which are only now and then in evidence,—a sphere in which, where all the nerve of sense is numb, in unconjectured bliss or in the abyss of ten-fold complicated change, the spirit itself may commune with others, " Spirit to Spirit, Ghost to Ghost " (*In Memoriam,* xciii) and do diverse wonders of which we are told in the volumes of the Society for Psychical Research, and which make us exclaim with Montaigne, " The spirit of man is a great worker of miracles."

Thirdly, the futile search of science for the spirits. It may be questioned whether more comfort or sorrow has come to the race since man peopled the unseen world with spirits to bless and demons to damn him. On the one hand, what more gracious in life than to think of a guardian spirit, attendant with good influences from the cradle to the grave, or that we are surrounded by an innumerable company from which we are shut off only by this muddy vesture of decay ? Perhaps they live in the real world,

* Henry More.

and we are in the shadow-land! Who
knows? Perhaps the poet is right :—

I tell you we are fooled by the eye, the ear :
These organs muffle us from that real world
That lies about us ; we are duped by brightness.
The ear, the eye doth make us deaf and blind ;
Else should we be aware of all our dead
Who pass above us, through us, and beneath us.
(Stephen Phillips, *Herod*).

If we had to do only with ministering
spirits, what a benign effect such a belief
might exercise, indeed has exercised, on the
minds of men ; but, alas ! there is another
side to the picture, and there is no blacker
chapter in our history than that in which is
told the story of the prince of the power of
the air and his legions. For weal or for woe
—who shall say the more potent ?—it is
impossible to over-estimate the importance
of this belief in a spirit-world.

The search of science for the spirits has
been neither long nor earnest ; nor is it a
matter of surprise that it has not been
undertaken earlier by men whose training
had fitted them for the work. It is no clear
vasty deep, but a muddy, Acheronian pool
in which our modern spirits dwell, with
Circe as the presiding deity and the Witch

125

of Endor as her high priestess. Commingling with the solemn incantations of the devotees who throng the banks, one can hear the mocking laughter of Puck and of Ariel, as they play among the sedges and sing the monotonous refrain, " What fools these mortals be." Sadly besmirched and more fitted for a sojourn in Anticyra than in Athens has been the condition of those who have returned from the quest,* and we cannot wonder that scientific men have hesitated to stir the pool and risk a touch from Circe's wand. All the more honour to those who have with honest effort striven to pierce the veil and explore the mysteries which lie behind it. The results are before us in the volumes of the Society for Psychical Research, and in the remarkable work of that earnest soul, F. W. H. Myers.[14] To enter upon a criticism of this whole question would be presumptuous. I have not had the special training which gives value to a judgment, but for many years I have had a practical interest in it, since much of my work is among the brothers of Sir Galahad, and the sisters of Sir Percival, among the

* *Anatomy of Melancholy,* Part II., Sect. 4.

dreamers of dreams and the seers of visions, whose psychical vagaries often transcend the bounds of every-day experiences. After a careful review of the literature, can an impartial observer say that the uncertainty has been rendered less uncertain, the confusion less confounded ? I think not.

> Dare I say
> No spirit ever brake the band
> That Stays him from the native land
> Where firSt he walk'd when claspt in clay ?
> (*In Memoriam*, xciii.)

Who dare say so ? But on the other hand, who dare affirm that he has a message from the spirit-land so legible and so sensible that the members of the National Academy of Sciences would convene to discuss it in special meeting ?

Fourthly, knowing nothing of an immortality of the spirit, science has put on an immortality of the flesh, and in a remarkable triumph of research has learned to recognise in every living being at once immortal age beside immortal youth. The patiently worked out Story of the morphological continuity of the germ plasm is one of the fairy tales of science. You who

127

listen to me to-day feel organised units in a
generation with clear-cut features of its own,
a chosen section of the finely woven fringe
of life built on the coral reef of past generations,—and, perhaps, if any, you, citizens
of no mean city, have a right to feel of some
importance. The revelations of modern
embryology are a terrible blow to this pride
of descent. The individual is nothing more
than the transient off-shoot of a germ plasm,
which has an unbroken continuity from
generation to generation, from age to age.
This marvellous embryonic substance is
eternally young, eternally productive, eternally forming new individuals to grow up
and to perish, while it remains in the progeny
always youthful, always increasing, always
the same. " Thousands upon thousands of
generations which have arisen in the course
of ages were its products, but it lives on in
the youngest generations with the power of
giving origin to coming millions. The
individual organism is transient, but its
embryonic substance, which produces the
mortal tissues, preserves itself imperishable,
everlasting, and constant." [15] This astonish-
ing revelation not only necessitates a re-
128

adjustment of our ideas on heredity, but it gives to human life a new and a not very pleasant meaning. It makes us "falter where we firmly trod" to feel that man comes within the sweep of these profound and inviolate biological laws, but it explains why nature—so careless of the single life, so careful of the type—is so lavish with the human beads, and so haphazard in their manufacture, spoiling hundreds, leaving many imperfect, snapping them and cracking them at her will, caring nothing if the precious cord on which they are strung—the germ plasm—remains unbroken. Science minimises to the vanishing-point the importance of the individual man, and claims that the cosmic and biological laws which control his destiny are wholly inconsistent with the special-providence view in which we were educated—that beneficent, fatherly providence which cares for the sparrows and numbers the very hairs of our head.

III

THE TERESIANS [16]

There remains for consideration the most interesting group of the three to the scientific student, representing the very opposite pole in life's battery, and either attracting or repelling, according as he has been negatively or positively charged from his cradle. There have always been two contending principles in human affairs, an old-time antagonism which may be traced in mythology and in the theologies, and which in philosophy is represented by idealism and realism, in every-day life by the head and the heart. Aristotle and Plato, Abelard and St. Bernard, Huxley and Newman, represent in different periods the champions of the intellect and of the emotions. Now on the question of the immortality of the soul, the only people who have ever had perfect satisfaction are the idealists, who walk by faith and not by sight. " Many are the wand bearers, few are the mystics," said Plato. " Many be called but few are chosen," said Christ. Of the hosts that cry,

130

Lord! Lord! few have that earnest expectation of the creature which has characterised in every age those strong souls laden with fire who have kept alive this sentiment of immortality—the little flock of Teresians, who feel that to them it is given to *know* the mysteries.*

Not always the wise men after the flesh (except among the Greeks), more often the lowly and obscure, women more often than men, these Teresians have ever formed the moral leaven of humanity. Narrow, prejudiced, often mistaken in worldly ways and methods, they alone have preserved in the past, and still keep for us to-day, the faith that looks through death. Children of Light, Children of the Spirit, whose ways are foolishness to the children of this world, mystics, idealists, with no strong reason for the faith that is in them, yet they compel admiration and imitation by the character of the life they lead and the beneficence of the influence they exert. The serene faith of Socrates with the cup of hemlock at his lips, the heroic devotion of a St. Francis or a St. Teresa, but more often for each one of us

* *Matthew* xiii. 11.

the beautiful life of some good woman
whose—

Eyes are homes of faithful prayer,

Whose loves in higher love endure.
(*In Memoriam*, xxxii.)

do more to keep alive among the Laodiceans a
belief in immortality than all the preaching in
the land. Some of you may recall how strongly
this is brought out in Cardinal Newman's
University Sermon, "Personal Influence,
the Means of Propagating the Truth." [17]

Though a little flock, this third group is
the salt of the earth, so far as preserving for
us a firm conviction of the existence of
another and a better world. Not by the
lips, but by the life, are men influenced in
their beliefs, and when reason calls in vain
and arguments fall on deaf ears, the still
small voice of a life lived in the full faith of
another may charm like the lute of Orpheus,
and compel an unwilling assent by a strong,
indefinable attraction, not to be explained in
words, outside the laws of philosophy, a
something which is not apparent to the
senses, and which is manifest only in its
effects. In that most characteristic Eastern

132

scene before King Darius (1 *Esdras*, iv), in the discussion, Which is the strongest thing in the world ? Zorobabel was right in giving woman the preëminence, since she is the incarnation of the emotional, of that element in life which sways like a reed the minds of men.

The remarkable development of the material side of existence may make us feel that Reason is King with science as the prime minister, but this is a most short-sighted view of the situation. To-day as always the heart controls, not alone the beliefs, but the actions of men, in whose life the head counts for little, partly because so few are capable of using their faculties, but more particularly because we are under the dominion of the emotions, and our deeds are the outcome of passion and prejudice, of sentiment and usage much more than of reason. From the standpoint of science, representing the head, there is an irreconcilable hostility to this emotional or cardiac side of life's problems, yet as one of the most important facts in man's history it has to be studied, and has been studied in a singularly lucid way in this University by one recognised everywhere as

a master in Israel.* Unfortunately, with the
heart man believeth, not alone unto righteousness, but unto every possible vagary,
from Apollonius of Tyana to Joseph Smith.
Where is the touchstone to which a man may
bring his emotions to the test, when, as the
great Stagirite remarks, ordinary opinions
are not less firmly held by some than positive
knowledge by others ? In our temporising
days man is always seeking a safe middle
ground between loyalty to the intellectual
faculty and submission to authority in an
unreasoning acceptance of the things of the
spirit. On the question of immortality the
only enduring enlightenment is through
faith. " Only believe," and " he that
believeth,"—these are the commandments
with comfort ; not " only think," and " he
that reasoneth," for these are the commandments of science. To many the awk-
wardness of the mental predicament would
be more keenly felt were it not for the
subtleness and suppleness of our under-
standing, which is double and diverse, just
as the matters are double and diverse.

Though his philosophy finds nothing to

* William James.

support it, at least from the standpoint of Terence the scientific student should be ready to acknowledge the value of a belief in a hereafter as an asset in human life. In the presence of so many mysteries which have been unveiled, in the presence of so many yet unsolved, he cannot be dogmatic and deny the possibility of a future state; and however distressing such a negative attitude of mind to the Teresian, like Pyrrho, he will ask to be left, reserving his judgment, but still inquiring. He will recognise that amid the turbid ebb and flow of human misery, a belief in the resurrection of the dead and the life of the world to come is the rock of safety to which many of the noblest of his fellows have clung; he will gratefully accept the incalculable comfort of such a belief to those sorrowing for precious friends hid in death's dateless night; he will acknowledge with gratitude and reverence the service to humanity of the great souls who have departed this life in a sure and certain hope—but this is all. Whether across death's threshold we step from life to life or whether we go, in the words of Job, whence we shall not return, even to the land

135

of darkness as darkness itself, he cannot tell. Nor is this strange. Science is organised knowledge, and knowledge is of things we see. Now the things that are seen are temporal ; of things that are unseen science knows nothing, and has at present no means of knowing anything.

The man of science is in a sad quandary to-day. He cannot but feel that the emotional side to which faith leans makes for all that is bright and joyous in life. Fed on the dry husks of facts, the human heart has a hidden want which science cannot supply ; as a steady diet it is too strong and meaty, and hinders rather than promotes harmonious mental metabolism. In illustration, what a sad confession that emotional Dryasdust, Herbert Spencer, has made in his *Autobiography*, when he admits that he preferred a third-rate novel to Plato, and that he could not read Homer ! Extremes meet. The great idealist would have banished poets from his Republic as teachers of myths and fables, and had the apostle of evolution been dictator of a new Utopia, his Index expurgatorius would have been still more rigid. To keep his mind sweet the modern scientific man should be saturated with the Bible and Plato, with Shakespeare, and Milton ; to see life through their eyes may enable him to strike a balance between the rational and the emotional, which is the most serious difficulty of the intellectual life.

A word in conclusion to the young men in the audience. As perplexity of soul will be your lot and portion, accept the situation with a good grace. The hopes and fears which make us men are inseparable, and this wine-press of Doubt each one of you must tread alone. It is a trouble from which no man may deliver his brother or make agreement with another for him. Better, as in Shelley's *Adonais*, that your spirit's bark be driven far from the shore, far from the trembling throng whose sails were never to the tempest given, than that you should tie it up to rot at some Lethean wharf. On the question before us, wide and far your hearts will range from those early days when matins and evensong, evensong and matins sang the larger hope of humanity into your young souls. In certain of you the changes and chances of the years ahead will reduce this to a vague sense of eternal continuity,

137

with which, as Walter Pater says, none of us wholly part. In a very few it will be begotten again to the lively hope of the Teresians ; while a majority will retain the sabbatical interest of the Laodicean, as little able to appreciate the fervid enthusiasm of the one as the cold philosophy of the other. Some of you will wander through all phases, to come at last, I trust, to the opinion of Cicero,* who had rather be mistaken with Plato than be in the right with those who deny altogether the life after death ; and this is my own *confessio fidei*.

Immortality is a complex problem, difficult to talk about, still more difficult to write upon with any measure of intelligence or consistency. Like Simias, in the Golden Dialogue † of the great master, a majority of sensible men will feel oppressed by the greatness of the subject and the feebleness of man, and it is with these feelings I close this simple objective statement of some of the existing conditions of thought.

* *Tusculan Disputations.*
† *Phædo.*

NOTES TO SCIENCE AND IMMORTALITY

1, p. 103.

" He gave the little wealth he had
    To build a house for fools and mad :
    And show'd by one satiric touch
    No nation wanted it to much."
            (*Verses on the death of Dr. Swift.*)

2, p. 105.

" I am a true labourer ; I earn that I eat, get that
I wear, owe no man hate, envy no man's happiness,
glad of other men's good, content with my harm,
and the greatest of my pride " (to paraphrase Corin's
words) " is to see my patients get well, and my
students work."

3, p. 109.

A friend (W. S. B.), thoroughly conversant with
Eastern life and thought, sends the following
criticism of this statement : " Jowett's mistake is
not his own. He merely repeats the usual Western
error of thinking—perhaps from the form of the
word—that Nirvana means annihilation in the sense
of destruction, whereas in the East they understand
by it annihilation through growth, in the sense in
which the seed is annihilated in the grown plant, the
ovum in the animal, or any germ or embryonic form

in its complete development. As the possible development of man is infinite, he is in the same way annihilated as man by growing to be co-extensive with the universe, which is the natural course of things according to the Eastern view,—the normal process of growth, which may be hastened intentionally if desirable."

4, p. 109.

Letters of a Chinese Official, 1902.

5, p. 110.

Nowhere is this philosophy of life so graphically described as in the Wisdom of Solomon, chapter ii. :

" Our life is short and tedious, and in the death of a man there is no remedy : neither was there any man known to have returned from the grave. For we are born at all adventure : and we shall be hereafter as though we had never been : for the breath in our nostrils is as smoke, and a little spark in the moving of our heart : which being extinguished, our body shall be turned into ashes, and our spirit shall vanish as the soft air. And our name shall be forgotten in time, and no man shall have our works in remembrance, and our life shall pass away as the trace of a cloud, and shall be dispersed as a mist, that is driven away with the beams of the sun, and overcome with the heat thereof. For our time is a very shadow that passeth away ; and after our end there is no returning : for it is fast sealed, so that no man cometh again. Come on therefore, let us enjoy the good things that are present, and let us speedily use the creatures like as in youth. Let us fill ourselves with costly wine and ointments : and let no flower of the spring pass by us : let us crown ourselves with rosebuds, before they be withered : let none of us go without his part of our voluptuousness : let us leave tokens of our joyfulness in every place : for this is our portion and our lot is this."

6, p. 111.

" The soul's dark cottage, batter'd and decay'd,
    Lets in new light, through chinks that Time hath
        made :
Stronger by weakness, wiser men become
As they draw near to their eternal home,
Leaving the old, both worlds at once they view
That stand upon the threshold of the new."
            (EDMUND WALLER, *Old Age.*)

7, p. 111.

Literary Friends and Acquaintance, 1902.

8, p. 112·

Literary Friends and Acquaintance, 1902.

9, p. 115.

Interstate Commerce Commission, Accident Bulletin, No. 8.

10, p. 115.

Statistics collected by the *Journal of the American Medical Association,* January 30, 1904.

141

11, p. 116.

" By brothers' blows, by brothers' blood,
Our souls are gashed and ſtained.
Alas ! What horror have we fled !
What crimes not wrought ?   What hath the dread
Of Heaven our youth reſtrained ? "
(HORACE, *Carmina*, i. 35, Theodore Martin's
Translation.)

12, p. 117.

" Dr. Howe's hand moved slowly back to the big
pocket in one of his black coat-tails, and brought
out a small, shabby prayer-book.

" ' You will let me read the prayers for the sick,'
he continued gently, and without waiting for a reply
began to say with more feeling than Dr. Howe often
put into the reading of the service,—

" ' Dearly beloved, know this, that Almighty God
is the Lord of life and death, and of all things to
them pertaining ; as '——

" ' Archibald,' said Mr. Denner faintly, ' you will
excuse me, but this is not—not necessary, as it
were.'

" Dr. Howe looked at him blankly, the prayer-
book closing in his hand.

" ' I mean,' Mr. Denner added, ' if you will allow
me to say so, the time for—for speaking thus has
passed.   It is now, with me, Archibald.'

" There was a wiſtful look in his eyes as he
spoke.

" ' I know,' answered Dr. Howe tenderly, thinking that the Visitation of the Sick muſt wait, ' but
God enters into now ; the Eternal is our refuge, a
very present help in time of trouble.'

" ' Ah—yes,' said the sick man ; ' but I should
like to approach this from our usual—point of view,

if you will be so good. I have every respect for your office, but would it not be easier for us to speak of—of this as we have been in the habit of speaking on all subjects, quite—in our ordinary way, as it were ? You will pardon me, Archibald, if I say anything else seems—ah—unreal ? ' "

When a recent well-known English bishop lay a-dying, his chaplain leaning over him said some soothing prayers, but—so the story goes—the bishop remarked, " Don't be a fool, H. ! Pass the syphon ! "

13, p. 123.

This it was which worried Henry More, the Platonist, whose treatise on the " Immortality of the Soul " is full of the wonders of the psychical research of that day. " For if we do but observe the great difference of our intellectual operations in infancy and dotage, from what they are when we are in the prime of our years ; and how that our wit grows up by degrees, flourishes for a time, and at last decays, keeping the same pace with the changes that age and years bring into our body, which observes the same laws that flowers and plants do ; what can we suspect, but that the soul of man, which is so magnificently spoken of amongst the learned, is nothing else but a temperature of body, and that it grows and spreads with it both in bigness and virtues, and withers and dies as the body does, or at least that it does wholly depend on the body in its operations, and that therefore there is no sense nor perception of anything after death ? " (*Works*, 4th ed., 1713, p. 225.)

14, p. 126.

Human Personality, London, 1903.

143

15, p. 128.

Noll, quoted by Beard, *Review of Neurology and Psychiatry*, January, 1904.

16, p. 130.

Saint Teresa, 1515–1582. In a paragraph before *A Hymn to the Name and Honour of the Admirable Saint Teresa*, Richard Crashaw thus describes her: " A woman, for angelical height of speculation, for masculine courage of performance, more than a woman, who yet a child outran maturity, and durst plot a martyrdom." In another poem he thus apostrophises her :—

" O thou undaunted daughter of desires
  By all thy dower of lights and fires ;
  By all the eagle in thee, all the dove ;
  By all thy lives and deaths of love ;
  By thy large draughts of intellectual day ;
  And by thy thirsts of love more large than they ;
  By all thy brim-fill'd bowls of fierce desire ;
  By thy last morning's draught of liquid fire ;
  By the full kingdom of that final kiss
  That seized thy parting soul, and seal'd thee his ;
  By all the Heavens thou hast in him
  (Fair sister of the seraphim) ;
  By all of him we have in thee ;
  Leave nothing of myself in me.
  Let me so read thy life, that I
  Unto all life of mine may die."

An excellent paper upon her life and work, by Annie Fields, appeared in the *Atlantic Monthly* for March, 1903. In an article, " L'Hystérie de Sainte Thérèse," in the *Archives de Neurologie*, 1902, Dr. Rouby gives an analysis of her life and writings from the standpoint of a modern scientific alienist.

17, p. 132.

" The men commonly held in popular estimation are greatest at a distance ; they become small as they are approached ; but the attraction exerted by un-conscious holiness is of an urgent and irresistible nature : it persuades the weak, the timid, the waver-ing, and the inquiring ; it draws forth the affection and loyalty of all who are in a measure like-minded ; and over the thoughtless or perverse multitude it exercises a sovereign compulsory sway, bidding them fear and keep silence, on the ground of its own right divine to rule them,—its hereditary claim on their obedience, though they understand not the principles or counsels of that spirit, which is born not of blood, nor of the will of the flesh, nor of the will of man, but of God."